THE
GREAT
AMERICAN
CAMPING
COOKBOOK

★

ICE BLINK: THE TRAGIC FATE OF SIR JOHN FRANKLIN'S
LOST POLAR EXPEDITION

ATLANTIC: THE LAST GREAT RACE OF PRINCES

>>>>><<<<<

Scott Cookman

>>>>>★<<<<<

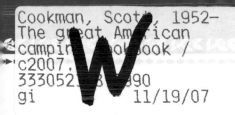

THE GREAT AMERICAN CAMPING COOKBOOK

BROADWAY BOOKS ◄••► NEW YORK

BROADWAY

PUBLISHED BY BROADWAY BOOKS

Published in the United States by Broadway Books,
an imprint of The Doubleday Broadway Publishing group,
a division of Random House, Inc., New York.
www.broadwaybooks.com

BROADWAY BOOKS and its logo, a letter B bisected on the diagonal,
are trademarks of Random House, Inc.

Book design by Elizabeth Rendfleisch
Illustrations by Rick Allen, Kenspeckle Letterpress

Library of Congress Cataloging-in-Publication Data
Cookman, Scott, 1952–
The great American camping cookbook / by Scott Cookman. —1st ed.
p. cm.
Includes bibliographical references and index.
1. Outdoor cookery. 2. Cookery, American. I. Title.
TX823.C634 2007
641.5'78—dc22
2006030528

ISBN: 978-0-7679-2308-8

PRINTED IN THE UNITED STATES OF AMERICA

1 3 5 7 9 10 8 6 4 2

First Edition

For my brothers, Pete and Whitney,
my sweet sister-in-law Susan and,
of course, my parents—
my guardian angels
in my own fight with cancer

Contents

PART VII ★ Spirits

OF CAMPS AND COOKING

The old ones, though you don't listen, know more than you.
If you listened, you would know it too and spare yourself the
labor of re-learning what is already known.
—OTTER, OJIBWAY ELDER, 1796

MY GRANDFATHER had a summer camp on Owasco Lake, in
the heart of New York's Finger Lakes region. To reach it you
quit the last of the paved road and turned onto a dirt one,
pungent with oil the county road crews laid to keep down
the summer dust. It descended a long slope toward the lake,
a cornfield on the right and dark woods on the left. The corn,
in August as tall as a man, smelled sweet and the woods as
yeasty as sourdough starter. At the foot of the slope, the road
made an abrupt left-hand turn into the oak and maple forest.
Under the shadows of the trees, ferns grew in profusion and
the land started to smell of water. A mile later, the road dead-
ended by the shimmering lake, my grandfather's white-
painted, green-awninged camp framed by giant willows.

By today's standards, it was a simple place: a frame cottage
with a living/dining area, two small bedrooms, tiny kitchen,

and even tinier bath. But it had a fine brick fireplace, big cushioned armchairs, built-in shelves heavy with books, walls hung with family photos and fishing and camp gear, big windows overlooking the lake, and—in and about every-thing—the scent of woodsmoke. Out front were a ram-shackle dock and a green-painted wooden boat named *Sagerjack*, with an outboard motor and varnished oars. In back was an old barn, with empty stalls and a tack room where my grandfather and his friends met weekly for poker games.

I remember watching in wonder as these camp games got under way. Big-finned cars pulled up, trunks yawned wide, and a Brobdingnagian feast materialized. It consisted of things strange and wonderful to my six-year-old eyes—clink-ing cases labeled Knickerbocker and Rheingold beer, and un-marked boxes filled with bottles of different shapes and colors. The green bottles, I was told, were gin; the brown ones rye; the amber ones Scotch or bourbon; the clear ones vodka. Other bottles contained stuff called tonic, seltzer, and mineral water, which sounded like medicines to me. In glass jars as big as my head were sauerkraut, pickles called "gorkies," green and black olives, red and yellow pickled pep-pers, and—most bizarre—pig's feet. Mesh sacks of what looked to me like ordinary onions were, I was told, "Vidalias," onions so sweet they could be eaten raw like apples.

I thought I'd seen hot dogs, cheese, and ham before. Hot dogs were skinny, pink, and plastic-wrapped; 12, all identical, in a pack. Cheese (Velveeta, the only approximation of cheese I'd ever tasted) was flame orange, soft as a slug, and came in a cardboard box. Ham was colorless, odorless, and came in an oval can. The hot dogs from the car trunks, however, called "brats," were obscenely fat, ghost-white, and strung together like links in a chain. The cheese from the trunks—white, not orange—was called "Cheddar" or "sharp" and came in wax-coated wheels. The hams didn't come in cans, but hung in what looked like fishing nets. They weren't colorless; rather, they were as dark as the mahogany of my grandfather's boat, smelled like burnt logs, and were called "smoked butts."

Red boxes of Ritz crackers and sacks of roasted peanuts in their shells, of course, I recognized at once. The buns for the brats, on the other hand, were altogether unfamiliar to me. They weren't light, sliced, and uniform in size or packaged in plastic bags like hot dog buns. They were heavy, unsliced loaves, bigger than cucumbers, piled in big brown paper bags with twine handles to carry the weight. When they were lifted and when they were dropped, they puffed flour, like smoke. The puffs smelled like a bakery.

The old men had all this food—which they called "chow"—organized and under way in remarkably short order. Charcoal and lighter fluid were put to work, pots and pans brought to the fore, and libations poured. The brats, pierced by forks or slashed with knives, were soon spitting on grills. The onions were sliced and laid thick in skillets to sizzle in butter. In a huge, galvanized stew pot set over coals, sauerkraut and chunks of smoked ham were brought to a boil and gobs of dough spooned on top to make dumplings. As things cooked, the men used their jackknives to cut wedges of Cheddar, spear "gorkies," and "noodle up" rings of peppers, and used their fingers to pluck ripe olives and pig's "knuckles" (no one called them feet) from jars. Each man sliced his own fresh-baked roll, seared its insides on a grill, filled it with a brat of his choosing, and slathered it to taste with smoking onions, hot mustard, or horseradish. From a ladle stuck in the stew pot, he served up whatever measure of kraut, butt, and dumplings he fancied.

Unlike any meal I'd ever seen, there was no apparent order to this eating except appetite, conviviality, and fellowship. There was certainly no single designated cook. All duties were shared. When one batch of brats was consumed, someone threw more on the grill and assumed stewardship over them until they were done. When the dumplings in the stew vanished, someone stirred up another batch of dough, plopped it in the pot, and watched over it until it was ready. Before the ice chests were emptied of cold beers, somebody would fetch a fresh case, put the cold ones on top, and pack the warm ones on the bottom so they would come up icy in turn. When supper was done—about full dark—dirty dishes and utensils were dropped into a waiting cauldron of scalding water somebody else had the forethought to prepare for the purpose. Everyone then adjourned to the tack room, lamps were lit, and pipe, cigar, and cigarette smoke filled the air.

As a child past bedtime, I was not admitted to this inner sanctum. But I had already witnessed and tasted the unadulterated feast of the Brobdingnagians. I went to sleep full and gloriously fed, as the sound of laughter and chinking poker chips echoed late into the night.

I have been hungry for camp food ever since.

◄ ◄ ◄ ACKNOWLEDGMENTS ►►►

I've never met a "chef" in camp, though I hope one day to be rich enough to afford one. Instead, I'm grateful to all the self-less, self-taught camp cooks who showed me how simple, easy, and fun camp cooking can be. Among them: "Cookie" Cookman, "Big Jim" Badonsky, Jim Clark, Dan Harrison, Gail Raeder, "Keefer" Fletcher, Dave Smith, "Long Tom" Lanners, "Kat" Toomey, Bill Lefferts, Sr., and, last, but not least, Greg Gates, whose spaghetti on a paper plate ringed with Oreo cookies was, indeed, a full-course meal. May we all meet again in the beautiful, out-of-the-way places.

THE
GREAT
AMERICAN
CAMPING
COOKBOOK

★

INTRODUCTION

The rock that wrecks most camping trips
is the cooking.

—ERNEST HEMINGWAY, 1922

A **GREAT DEAL** has changed—and a great deal hasn't—since Hemingway's time.

More Americans are flocking to the back-country than ever before. In fact, according to the Travel Industry of America, camping is now America's most popular outdoor activity. Nearly one quarter of the U.S. population—more than 65 million people—go camping every year. Some go on foot, with rucksacks on their backs; others by canoe or kayak; countless others by car.

All of them—as in Hemingway's time—still must necessarily cook for themselves. The vast majority—through inexperience, impatience, and no fault of their own—continue to do it badly.

They routinely take too much food or too little, usually of the wrong kind. They abandon fresh foods—the soul of American camp cooking—for processed ones. They assume "instant" foods are good, "no cook" foods are better, and that foods involving preparation are best left behind. Unpracticed at cooking over wood fires, they build bonfires to make bacon and eggs. Unused to camp stoves, they overcook fish and boil coffee into tar. Those cumulative culinary disasters ruin more camping vacations than any other cause.

It doesn't have to be that way.

The secret to great American camp cooking today is using the fresh, natural "comfort foods" of the good old days. Indeed, traditional American camp cooking is as varied, distinctive, and epicurean as any Old World or New Age cuisine. Few today realize that clambakes, succotash, country ham, baked beans, cornbread, roast turkey, wild rice, squash, potatoes, tomatoes, sourdough bread, tortillas, even Thousand Island dressing (to name a minimal few) are original American camp dishes. Fewer still remember how good and easy they are to make.

This book dishes up the rich history and the lost art of American camp cooking in more than a hundred delicious, easy-to-make, traditional recipes. It offers a broad range of dishes: some for backpackers, others for canoeists, and still others for car campers. All of them, however, feature fresh or naturally preserved foods. The real stuff. The good stuff. The stuff of camp memories.

Whether camp is a comfortable weekend cottage, a rustic hunting or fishing cabin, or a primitive canoeing or back-packing bivouac, *The Great American Camping Cookbook* offers easy, practical, and proven advice for unforgettable eating in the wild.

PART I

The Way It Was

★ CHAPTER 1 ★

DINING WITH SAVAGES

This is truly the land of Epicures.
—ARTIST GEORGE CATLIN, 1832

⇒★

IN THE WINTER of 1609–1610, when England's first colonists were starving to death at Jamestown, Virginia, Captain John Smith trekked to the nearest Native American village to beg, barter—or steal—food. "Extreme wind, rain, frost and snow caused us to keep Christmas amongst the Savages," he gloomily recorded in his diary, expecting little. To his amazement, the "Savages" (Powhatans) proved lavishly generous and gregarious hosts. "We were never [made] more merry, nor fed on more good oysters, fish, flesh, wild fowl and good bread," he wrote, "nor ever had better fires in England than in their dry, warm, smoky houses."

In fact, if Smith's and other contemporary accounts are accurate, he feasted on choice Chesapeake or Chincoteague oysters up to one foot long. Blue crabs were so big that "one provided a feast for four men." Fish included gourmet-caliber sea trout, weakfish, bluefish, and channel bass (red drum), some in excess of 40 pounds. Smith and his men were served venison loins, spit-roasted and seasoned with the black, sodium-rich residue of boiled-down hickory bark, which substituted admirably for salt. Leaner cuts were basted with clear bear fat or served with a dipping sauce made of "no end of oil from walnuts and acorns, which they know how to extract very well." Fat ducks and geese were plentiful.

The "good bread" Smith noted was made of a grain he'd never seen before—corn—ground into fine meal; mixed with boiling water, walnut oil, and dried berries into a stiff dough; wrapped in leaves; and baked in hot coals. For dessert, there were sunflower seeds and hickory nuts—altogether new to him—as well as "Very sweet" chestnuts. Afterward, the Powhatans invited him to smoke the cured leaves of a small, hardy native tobacco plant (*Nicotiana rustica*) that, soon exported to Europe, proved to be the salvation of Jamestown.

Stuffed, Smith and his men returned to the colony. By spring of 1610, subsisting on food bartered or taken outright from the natives, they were among the last 60 colonists—of the original 215—left alive.

This same scenario played itself out repeatedly among the first Europeans to penetrate the North American wilderness. Much to their astonishment, they found the natives' food and cooking far better, more varied, and infinitely healthier than their own.

Hernando de Soto and his Spanish conquistadors, who rampaged through the American Southeast in search of gold a half-century before Smith's Englishmen arrived at Jamestown, learned this lesson quickly. De Soto's nine ships landed 600 men at Tampa Bay in the spring of 1539. They carried with them over a year's worth of state-of-the-art, preserved European provisions: salted beef, pork, and herring; wheat flour in watertight casks; barrels of rice and dried peas; and kegs of onions, cabbage, and turnips pickled in brine. To furnish fresh meat on the hoof, they brought a herd of live cattle and a dozen pigs, the latter the first seen on the North American continent.

It did them little good. The salted meat and pickled vegetables, leached of vitamins and nutrients, resulted in scurvy. In Florida's heat and humidity, the flour and peas went blue-black with mold and swarmed with weevils. Without forage, the cattle soon died. About all that remained were the swine, which de Soto jealously guarded as his last-resort, emergency provisions.

In ruthless fashion, he fed his expedition off native foods plundered from the Indians. Foremost among these was corn: "Yellow for ordinary eating," according to the expedition's diarist, "and white for flour, which made very fine bread." Indeed, this native-grown grain, which contained more calories than the Spaniards' wheat flour, fuelled their march. So did other strange, but delectable, foods. From "the Savage's many fine fields, some a league [five miles] in extent," they looted mountains of beans, squash, and pumpkins—vegetables unknown in Europe, but rich in the nutrients, especially vitamins, their salt-cured provisions lacked. Taking native chiefs hostage along the way, they extorted huge quantities of other foodstuffs as well. "One chief," the diarist recorded, "sent two thousand bearers loaded with rabbits, partridges, corn cakes and many dogs," the latter esteemed a great delicacy. Another, held at swordpoint in modern-day South Carolina, "made a gift of 700 turkeys," a bird unknown to the Spaniards but domesticated by the natives, whose flesh made fine eating and whose feathers made light, warm down blankets.

Hostage-taking supplied de Soto with a galaxy of equally

exotic foods. There were potatoes, which the conquistadors called "earth apples," heartily disliked, and used primarily to feed their 113 war horses. There were sweet potatoes—not really potatoes, but roots related to the morning glory family—which they ate with great enthusiasm for their sugariness. There were bushels of altogether unfamiliar, yet delicious nuts, including pecans, peanuts, black walnuts, and hickory nuts. High in fat, they were greedily devoured right out of their shells or—pressed of their fine, clear oil by the Indians—used for shortening, frying, and baking. There were also baskets overflowing with fine, succulent grapes unknown in Europe—thick-skinned, seed-filled muscadines, Catawbas, and Concords. While the natives ate them fresh or dried, the Spaniards eagerly fermented them into a rough but swillable wine. In addition to grapes, there were wild plums, strawberries ("Finer and more delicate than those in Europe," according to the chronicler), mulberries, tart persimmons, wild spinach, purslane, and wild onions.

By robbing the Indians, de Soto survived handsomely for three years in the wilderness. He did not, however, survive the bloody trail he'd left behind. Near today's Mobile, Alabama, his freebooters were attacked and nearly wiped out by Native American Mobilians. With the remnant of his force, he battled the native Chickasaws across modern-day Mississippi. In 1542, he died—not of starvation, scurvy, or any dietary deficiency disease, but of yellow fever–bearing mosquitoes on the banks of the Mississippi River. He never found the gold he was looking for. He could never have imagined that the foods laid on his table represented a mother lode far richer.

Far to the north, Europeans still found fine eating. Even among the hunter-gatherer peoples of the interior, the variety and sophistication of New World cuisine more than equaled that of the Old.

On his epic canoe crossing of North America in 1792, explorer Alexander Mackenzie set out with typical voyageur's provisions: dried peas, premade ship's biscuit (hardtack), and casks of salted pork. The ultralight, long-life rations of their day, they provided a regular, but relentlessly monotonous menu: hardtack and raw pork while underway, pea and pork porridge thickened with broken hardtack at night. Luckily, Mackenzie found himself lavishly feasted by scores of Native American nations on his journey west. Indeed, his journal constitutes something of a gastronomic cross-section of the continent at the time—a "foodie's" memoir, if there ever was one.

Around the Great Lakes, the Ottawa (reputed to be the finest canoemen and anglers on the lakes) treated him to "fat [lake] trout," "exquisite" whitefish, and "handsomely smoked sturgeon." Considering the lake trout were up to five feet long and the sturgeon as much as ten, the bounty was even more impressive. West of Lake Superior, the Ojibway regaled him with "wild rice sweetened with [maple] sugar." This grain, as unique to America as corn, was not only gourmet fare, but spectacularly nutritious, with twice the protein, double the iron, and more than ten times the vitamins of brown rice. Stewed with native-made maple sugar, it made a near-perfect, balanced "power meal" that happily propelled Mackenzie and his paddlers west.

Along the forested rivers and lakes of the interior, the Assiniboine treated him to roast bear liver "wrapped in caul fat"; beaver tails, skinned like fish and broiled over coals; muskrat "fried in pieces, like chicken"; and the native's ultimate specialty: boiled moose nose. Mackenzie tasted the latter nervously, expecting a gelatinous mess. To the contrary, he found that the tip of the nose, sliced thin, consisted of delicate white meat, and the jowls a rich dark meat. He declared it "fine" and asked for more.

When he reached the Pacific coast, his Nootka hosts presented him an appetizer of "a large dish of salmon roes, pounded fine and beat up with water, so to give it the appearance of cream." This was followed by more salmon roe, mixed with gooseberries and sorrel leaves, which, Mackenzie recorded, added a distinct sweet-and-sour flavor to the salty eggs. For main courses, there were massive fillets of prime salmon, roasted, smoked, or boiled into rich chowder. For dessert, there were baskets overflowing with huckleberries and raspberries, "the finest I ever saw or tasted," he wrote. On his return trip, Mackenzie found he'd lost all appetite for hardtack and rancid salt pork.

Lewis and Clark, traversing the continent farther south in 1804–1806, met with an even greater gustatory variety. Wintering among the Mandan on the Missouri River, they eagerly traded iron, lead, and the services of their blacksmith for native-grown produce. This bought them Arikara yellow beans, Hidasta shield beans, Mandan bride corn, Chippewa corn, Algonquian pumpkin, Indian (Sibley) squash, and Seneca sunflower seeds. The corn and beans, boiled together, made succotash, an ideally balanced protein and carbohydrate meal. Dried pumpkin was boiled, mashed, and whipped into succulent purees or soups. More frequently, however, during the long Dakota winter, the expedition used it as a natural sweetener for "flip": a mixture of whiskey and water brought to a frothy boil with the insertion of a red-hot iron. The sunflower seeds were either pressed into a fine cooking oil or ground into rich flour.

The explorers gorged on buffalo, the mainstay of the prairie, prepared in half a hundred native ways, the choicest parts being the hump and the tongue. "The upper hump of the bison, weighing four or five pounds," wrote one explorer, "is called by the Indians the 'little hump.' This is usually of a harder, more compact nature than the rest and is usually put aside for keeping. The lower, larger part is streaked with fat and is very juicy and delicious. These are considered the delicacies." The tongue, however, was generally thought the ultimate morsel. It was soaked in water for 24 hours, boiled slowly for six, along with wild onions and herbs, then fried in what was called "prairie butter," or buffalo marrow. An even richer rich dish, a soup of buffalo blood and marrow, left the explorers "ashine with grease and gladness."

Crossing the Rockies, the expedition gratefully traded with the Nez Perce for camas—"a small, roundish root about the size of a small Irish potato," wrote Clark, "which the natives roast in the embers until soft. It has a very agreeable taste and answers very well in place of bread." Fermented, according to Clark, it also made "a verry [sic] good beer."

Wintering on the Pacific coast, the explorers developed a similar appetite for the foods of the native Clatsop. They traded their diminished stock of goods for immense quantities of fresh, dried, and smoked salmon, halibut, clams, whale meat, and smelt. Of all these, Clark, a man who'd experienced a continent's worth of the finest native fare, judged the tiny candlefish, or eulachon (a smelt), the most noteworthy of all. "I found them best when cooked in Indian stile [sic]," he wrote, "roasting a number of them together on a wooden spit, without any previous preparation whatever. They are so fat they require no additional sauce. I think them superior to any fish I ever tasted, even more delicate and lussious [sic] than the whitefish of the Great Lakes, heretofore my standard for excellence among the fishes." Pressed of their oil, the candefish furnished a rich dipping sauce for lean, winter-starved elk meat. The surplus oil fuelled the expedition's lamps, affording Lewis and Clark light to keep their journals.

The artist George Catlin, who first painted the Native Americans of the high plains some 25 years after Lewis and Clark's expedition, found Indian food—and hospitality—

equally memorable. In 1832, among the Mandan on the upper Missouri River, he was invited to a simple lunch. In a lodge 50 feet in diameter, he was seated on finely woven, multicolored rush mats laid with "handsome crockery bowls and buffalo horn spoons, polished bright as silver." He wrote that "the simple feast which was spread before us consisted of stewed pemmican [dried, shredded buffalo meat, pounded fine, larded with fat and marrow], a fine brace of buffalo ribs, delightfully roasted, and a kind of paste or pudding, made of the flour of the *pomme blanche,* as the French [traders] call it, a delicious turnip of the prairie [Jerusalem artichokes], finely flavored with buffalo berries." For dessert, he was presented with "great quantities of wild fruit—service berries, strawberries and wild plums." He ate his fill and confessed to his diary afterward: "This is truly the land of Epicures."

The abundance, variety, and gustatory goodness of Native American cuisine impressed other whites as well. At Christmas in 1845 another wayward artist named Paul Kane, crossing the continent by canoe and dog sled to paint Indians, found himself marooned by deep snow at the Hudson Bay Company's (HBC) remote outpost at Fort Edmonton in Alberta, Canada. The company-supplied fare at such posts— the HBC being notoriously cheap—was unrelievedly monotonous. Expecting a dismal meal of ossified salt beef and corn gruel, Kane wrote: "About two o'clock on Christmas Day, we sat down to dinner."

His mood improved following a "regale"—a full eight-ounce mug—of 100-proof brandy. He was surprised to see the table heaped with fresh native foods. "At the head of the table was a large dish of boiled buffalo hump," he noted, "[while] at the foot smoked a [whole] boiled buffalo calf." The sight of the latter unnerved him. But his host assured him to "fret not, the calf is very small and is taken from the cow by Caesarian operation long before it attains full growth.

This, boiled whole, is one of the most esteemed dishes among epicures of the interior." Indeed he was told it was equivalent to a "suckling pig of the plains" and fine eating, which he quickly found it was.

There was no formality about the feast. Everyone at the table tucked into it family-style. "My pleasing duty," Kane wrote, "was to help a dish of mouffle, or dried moose nose [a native specialty]. The gentleman on my left distributed whitefish, delicately browned in buffalo marrow. The priest served the buffalo tongue, while the chief trader cut up beavers' tails. The other gentleman at the table was occupied in dissecting a roast wild goose. The center of the table was graced with piles of potatoes, turnips [Jerusalem artichokes] and Indian [corn] bread."

Like Captain John Smith's, some 250 years before, it was the finest Christmas dinner Kane ever remembered.

★ CHAPTER 2 ★

FOOD CRIMES

How the Good Went Bad

The misery: who has forgotten it? Smoke from the fire everywhere, the coffeepot melted down, the can of soup upset in the fire and the exhausted victim—a piece of hardtack in one hand and a slice of canned beef in the other—dreaming of hot biscuits and juicy steaks.

—FOREST AND STREAM, 1920

THE GOODNESS of original camp cooking lies in fresh or naturally preserved foods. In the 1840s, however, not long after Paul Kane's never-forgotten holiday feast, all that changed. Convenience—technology disguised as progress—killed traditional camp cookery. And just about everyone's appetite.

Of Cans and Camp

It began with the introduction of canned foods. These were originally developed in 1798 by a Frenchman named Nicolas Appert, not to feed campers, but Napoleon's fast-marching, far-ranging armies. Fruits, vegetables, and meats were cooked at high temperature in glass jars and sealed with cork stoppers. The cooking destroyed many of the harmful bacteria that often contaminated fresh foods and the airtight seal prevented any chance of recontamination. Unfortunately, cooking also destroyed much of the vitamin content—as well as the color, texture, and taste—of fresh foods. To bring out what natural color and flavor remained, as well as to retard the growth of any bacteria that had survived cooking, copious quantities of salt were added.

To test his new process, 18 varieties of Appert's preserved foods—mostly root vegetables—were delivered to the French navy. After 130 days at sea, they were opened and sampled. "Every one had retained its freshness," Appert wrote glowingly, "and not a single substance had undergone the least change at sea." At the time, everyone accepted this as a great advance: especially the emperor, who personally awarded Appert a prize of 12,000 francs (equivalent to roughly US $50,000 today).

In fact, virtually all the valuable attributes of fresh foods had been cooked or salted out of Appert's provisions. It was hardly surprising they survived their brief sea trial unchanged. There was nothing much good left in them to go bad. Indeed, as is now known, from 60 to 80 percent of nutrients are lost during the canning process. Nutritionally, Appert's canned cabbage, onions, and cucumbers were far inferior to those pickled in brine, which—uncooked, uncanned, and consequently far cheaper—easily kept up to six months. Root vegetables of the kind Appert canned—carrots, turnips, parsnips—kept that long in peasants' cellars, vitamins and flavor intact, with no adulteration whatever. So did dried vegetables, meat, and fish, which lasted twelve months or more.

What won Appert the prize—and his process notoriety—was the assumption that foods sealed in airtight containers kept indefinitely. As we now know, this was egregiously false. Even today's highly advanced canned foods have a shelf life ranging from as little as 18 months to a maximum of about five years, with three years a rough average. But given the emperor's appellation, canned foods were adopted for French army use.

From the outset, they did not sit well on Gallic palates. "Eating Monsieur Appert's [salted] comestibles is a biblical experience," wrote one French officer. "Afterwards one feels like Lot's wife." Another dourly noted: "If its issue [canned provisions] has advanced anything, it is the celerity with which troops strip the countryside of every alternative." Despite this, the emperor's enemies, Great Britain especially, adopted canned foods too. Something of an arms race—foodwise—resulted.

The British quickly discarded glass containers as too vulnerable to breakage for military use and substituted tin-plated cans. Manufacture of such new unbreakable containers, however, was by no means well understood, perfected, or systematic. There was no machinery for fabricating cans at the time, no automation whatever, so each can was made by hand (an exacting 16-step process). A skilled tinsmith could produce only about ten cans a day. This made tin-canned foods frightfully expensive, even by today's standards. In the early 1800s, for example, figured in current dollars, a one-pound tin of peas cost $3.36; a one-quart tin of vegetable soup $8.40; and a one-pound tin of potted beef $10.08! For the most part, demand for such costly tinned provisions was fueled by the navies of the world. Their expense was secondary to their immunity to breakage and spoilage, critical to sustaining extended cruises. The dual economy of minimal fuel and time required in their preparation—the original "heat and eat" foods—was an added attraction.

British seamen, however, complained about tinned provisions more mightily than Napoleon's soldiers ever did about those canned in glass. Indeed, in pursuit of a perfect, bombproof food package, nineteenth-century food engineers unwittingly fabricated near-perfect food bombs. Glass is chemically inert to all types of food. The metals used in tin-plated cans at the time—sheet iron, lead, tin, zinc, arsenic— decidedly aren't. In contact with food, they can discolor, contaminate, or outright poison it: sometimes all three. Glass, of course, admits light, which not only makes foods stored in it visible to inspection, but retards the growth of a number of pathogenic, light-hating microorganisms. Newly invented tin cans, on the other hand, soldered shut, left well-meaning food inspectors—and some very nasty bacteria—completely in the dark.

All this came shockingly to light in Great Britain in 1852. Complaints about tinned provisions supplied to the Royal Navy became so loud and widespread that a full-fledged Parliamentary investigation was ordered. At Portsmouth, Admiralty examiners duly struck open (with hammers and chisels, since the can opener had yet to be invented) a sampling of 306 large cans of meats and vegetables supplied to the navy. According to the *Illustrated London News:* "The stench arising from them was so great that it was impossible for the officials to carry out their duty without frequent and copious supplies of chloride of lime to the floor. Now and then a canister would emit such an odious stench as to cause all operations to be suspended for some minutes, and one was so overpowering that the examiners had to beat a hasty retreat from the room."

Out of all cans the examiners sampled, only 42 were judged remotely edible. The other 264 (fully 86 percent) were taken out to sea and sunk in the English Channel.

The investigation resulted in greater oversight of canned foods, with the Admiralty acting as something of a nineteenth-century Food and Drug Administration, so far as truth in labeling and food safety were concerned. Manufacturers vying for rich military contracts, in Great Britain and elsewhere, cleaned up their acts and their products.

By the 1860s, advances in canning technology had improved quality and reduced costs to an extent that such "militarized" provisions were widely marketed to the public. At first, these consisted of delicacies like tinned salmon, oysters, tomatoes, apricots, and peaches, which campers were delighted to have and happy to pay a premium to get, for their variety if nothing else.

In the 1870s, John Boyle O'Reilly, who first popularized recreational canoeing in America, paddled the Connecticut River with a companion and a "copious larder" of such luxuries. Among its contents were tinned tapioca, sardines, turtle soup, and potted shrimp. Interestingly, O'Reilly ate little of this canned fare. Instead he shrewdly traded it with farmers along the river for "quarts of fresh milk, butter, eggs and loaves of fresh-baked bread." By the 1880s, canned staples like corned beef, pork and beans, and condensed milk were common in camp. Indeed, by 1888, when H. J. Heinz introduced his "57 Varieties" of canned foods, cans had become ubiquitous. As early as 1890 the *Atlantic Monthly* was complaining that the high peaks of the Adirondacks were "strewn with campers' paper collars [gentlemen campers, at the time, attached disposable white paper collars to their shirts] and tin cans."

The fact that canned goods were largely water and therefore heavier than their traditional dried, smoked, or bulk-packed equivalents mattered little. Neither did the fact that they were still several orders of magnitude more expensive. The fact that they were the latest thing—ready-to-eat and warranted to keep indefinitely—outweighed all else.

While many prominent turn-of-the-century outdoorsmen complained about the new provisions, they toted them nonetheless. George Washington Sears, a writer for *Forest and Stream* at the time, wrote: "I carry my duffel in a light, pliable knapsack, and there is an aggravating antagonism between the uncompromising rims of a fruit-can, and the knobs of my vertebrae, that 20 years of practice have utterly failed to reconcile. And yet, I have found my account in a can of condensed milk . . . And I have found a small can of Boston baked beans a most helpful lunch, with a nine-mile portage ahead. It was not Epicurean, but had staying qualities."

Former president Teddy Roosevelt, a gargantuan eater who relished good food in camp (on a weekend camping trip in Yosemite with John Muir in 1903, he insisted on bringing along two cooks), took nothing but canned foods on his 1913–1914 "River of Doubt" expedition through the Brazilian rainforest. In fact, he packed a three-month supply consisting entirely of canned foods: beef, bacon, mutton, sausages, hard bread, potatoes, beans, and carrots. He had no illusions about the flavor of such stuff. In Cuba during the Spanish-American War in 1898, he'd come to hate it. He called canned boiled beef "stringy, tasteless and disagreeable in appearance," and canned mutton simply "inedible." Consequently, he took along a prodigious variety of canned condiments to "correct them": chutney, horseradish, mustard, capers, shrimp sauce, lobster sauce, anchovies, curry powder, and cayenne.

Roosevelt had all these cans packed into 90 larger, watertight cans, each holding a day's rations for five men. In event of emergency, he also took along 75 of the U.S. Army's newly invented "iron rations": each ration consisted of a one-pound tin of corned beef and two 8-ounce tins of hardtack, calculated to sustain a man for one day. Roosevelt also packed three bottles of Scotch whiskey, secured in a watertight can of their own and carefully wrapped in blankets. None of the canned food was embarked for its culinary merits, but for insurance. It was fuel. Indeed, the canned provisions saved Roosevelt and his whole party from starvation on their near-disastrous 60-day wilderness descent of what is today called the Rio Roosevelt.

During World War I, an entire generation of farm-fed Americans (nearly 5 million served in the last 19 months of the conflict) was weaned from fresh to canned food. A typical daily supply requisition for the 1.3 million–man U.S. Army in France, dated August 11, 1918, included 1,250,000 cans of tomatoes, 900,000 cans of pork and beans, 750,000 cans of hash, 600,000 cans of corned beef, and 400,000 cans of evaporated milk. When the doughboys came home, the canned food habit came with them.

Author Ernest Hemingway epitomized the change in taste. On his return from World War I, he went camping in Michigan. He filled his pack with canned spaghetti, canned pork and beans, condensed milk, and canned apricots. "I've got a right to eat this kind of stuff," he wrote, "if I'm willing to carry it."

Emergency army rations—combining maximum calories, minimum weight, and minimal preparation—also became popular with campers. Among these was German-developed erbwurst, also called "dynamite soup," since it consisted of a stick of dehydrated, compressed peameal that required only boiling water to render into a flavorless, somewhat gagging meal. Oddly, it became a favorite of early Appalachian Trail hikers, more for its "hair shirt" than culinary appeal. Another was the British army's canned meat and vegetable mixture called Maconachie, after its manufacturer. It was promoted as "the ideal ration . . . prepared in a few moments . . . a little goes a very long way." No doubt a little certainly went a long way. Maconachie consisted of sliced turnips and carrots, swimming in a thin, gray, fat-globuled gravy of indeterminate origin. "Warmed in the tin, it was edible," wrote one soldier. "Cold it was a mankiller."

Nonetheless, these and various other newly engineered "food products" found their way into the packbaskets and rucksacks of nouveau-riche outdoorsmen in the 1920s. Among them were instant coffee (a dry concentrate), artificial cheese (made from vegetable oil, with not a particle of milk), condensed soups, and "concentrated meat" (a pressed amalgamation of beef powder and cooked wheat). None of these were anywhere near as good or healthy as their fresh counterparts. All, however, represented the height of convenience at the time. This novelty, not to mention the products' macho military origins, made them ruggedly fashionable.

By the same irrational dynamic—from the Great War to the latest Gulf War—highly processed military rations, or their quickly spun-off civilian counterparts, all but crowded fresh foods, any notion of cooking, and any need for cooks out of camp. The twentieth-century food engineers took over. Their inventions shared three characteristics: they required no preparation whatever, could be eaten hot or cold, and kept virtually forever. None of these rendered them remotely gustatory.

The ubiquitous C-ration, the result of U.S. Army experiments begun in 1938, fed three generations of servicemen in World War II, Korea, and Vietnam—an incredible 31 million in all. Unlike earlier canned foods, leeched of natural vitamins and minerals during cooking, the C-ration was fortified with synthetically made ones. It came neatly packed in six cans and was intended to provide a soldier—according to the army—with "three full, satisfying meals a day."

It was certainly filling. A day's worth of C-rations weighed over five pounds and contained a whopping 4,437 calories. Culinarily, it was hardly satisfying. Three cans contained processed meat products ("M-components") and three cans contained processed bread products ("B-components"). The labeling of meat and bread as food products, not food, marked a rather slippery culinary divide. A typical day's ration (Menu #1, in army quartermaster's jargon) included one can of mixed ham, egg, and potato product; one can of pork and beans; and one can of chicken and vegetable product (the meat components). The bread components consisted of one can of premixed, compressed dry cereal; one can of hard bread; and one can containing instant coffee, sugar cubes, and chocolate-coated peanuts.

A soldier, using a tiny, folding P-4 can opener (usually strung on a chain with his dog tags), could open these cans and eat them whenever he was hungry or, more typically, whenever time allowed. Veteran troopers habitually carried but one eating utensil: a spoon, inserted through the buttonhole of a shirt flap, the shaft secured in the pocket. Indeed, the two things no veteran ever lost—if he hoped to eat— were his spoon and can opener. The problem with C-rations, as with all canned foods in the field, was weight. Initially, the six cans comprising a day's ration weighed 15 ounces apiece (nearly 6 pounds total), and although this was soon reduced to 12 ounces apiece (4$\frac{1}{2}$ pounds total), it was still too much. As newspaper correspondent Ernie Pyle, who soldiered alongside the infantry in World War II, recorded: "Each night enough canned rations for three days are brought up across country in jeeps, but when the men move on after supper, most of them either 'lose' or leave behind the next days' rations because they're too heavy to carry."

The K-ration, initially developed for paratroops, but later almost universally supplied to soldiers on the front lines in lieu of C-rations, was lighter, more individualized, and even more convenient. It was packaged in three slim, self-contained, wax-coated boxes plainly labeled breakfast, dinner, or supper. Breakfast consisted of a tuna-sized can of egg and meat product (with attached opening key—no need of a can opener); four hard crackers (little better than the hardtack of the Civil War); a dried fruit bar; instant coffee, sugar, and a wooden spoon (no need to carry a metal one); four cigarettes; Dentyne chewing gum; water purification tablets; and toilet paper. Dinner (lunch) was a tuna-sized can of processed cheese, with opening key; another four hard crackers; a chocolate bar; lemon, orange, or grape juice powder; four more cigarettes; a book of matches; and salt tablets. Supper featured a tuna-sized can of "meat product," another four hard crackers, another chocolate bar, a packet of bouillon soup powder, four more cigarettes, more chewing gum, and another issue of toilet paper. The wax cartons in which each meal was packed were designed to burn long enough to heat a canteen cup of coffee or soup.

The D-ration—the last-ditch, emergency combat ration—was the precursor of today's "power bars." By regulation, every soldier carried one. Fortified with vitamins, it was an amalgamation of chocolate, sugar, milk powder, cocoa fat, oat flour, and vanilla flavoring. A marvel of food engineering at the time, it weighed only four ounces and contained 600 calories. Rock-hard and thoroughly unappetizing, it was seldom eaten.

FREEZE-DRIED FALLACIES

The introduction of long-range reconnaissance patrol (LRRP) rations during the Vietnam War either revolutionized or ruined (depending upon your interpretation) eating in the field. These were among the first modern freeze-dried foods. The ancient Incas of the Andes had actually pioneered the reverse process a millennia or more earlier to make *charqui*. In the thin, dry air of the high mountains, they laid strips of meat in the sun to slowly evaporate moisture during the day, then left them out overnight to fast-freeze. The fast-freeze preserved the meat's natural cellular structure—and thereby its original taste, texture, and nutritive benefit—while desiccating it almost entirely. Rid of water, the meat was impervious to spoilage. Undamaged by cooking or any additives, it was near perfectly preserved fresh food.

In the modern version, processed meat and vegetables (vitamin fortified, sodium laced, and artificially colored) are flash frozen in a vacuum, then mildly heated (not cooked, mind you) to sublimate water content. The process, though expensive, effectively dries and compacts foods to about one-third to one-quarter of the weight and volume of canned rations. Logistically, of course, this made freeze-dried foods ideal for military use. Morale-wise, they seemed equally advanced. Rehydrated (using another Vietnam-era advance, the two-quart, collapsible canteen) and heated over solid fuel (hexamine) tablets, they had pretty much the flavor and form of fresh food.

The trade-offs, however, quickly became apparent. Freeze-dried rations were comparatively lower in calories and even higher in salt than their canned equivalents. To render them edible, the water removed in their factory processing had to be replaced in the field, where fresh water was always scarce. To make bad water good required chlorine-liberating halazone tablets, which took a good 30 minutes to purify one quart, and imbued the food with the swimming pool–aftertaste of chlorine. Alternatively, impure water could be boiled for 10 minutes in a GI's aluminum canteen cup to render it safe. This cup, unimproved since World War I, held 8 ounces. To reconstitute a freeze-dried ration required boiling two cups' worth of water (16 ounces), in sequence, which took a minimum of 20 minutes and considerable effort and fuel. Once the water, half-lukewarm and half-hot, was mixed with the ration, a trooper had to wait another 10 minutes, stirring constantly, before it was palatable. Few of the "lurps" (LRRP troopers) who had to subsist on this stuff for weeks at a time in the highlands of Vietnam ever wanted to see it or eat it again.

Promoted at home in the 1960s, however—about the same time that ultralight, synthetic materials revolutionized design of tents, backpacks, and sleeping bags—campers flocked to buy its brightly packaged, relabeled civilian equivalents. The sales pitch was compelling enough to make them forget its expense. Who could resist a freeze-dried dinner that weighed only 4 ounces and, reconstituted with boiling water, made a 20-ounce meal for two? By the same token, what party of two, off for a week afoot in the wild, wouldn't be delighted that a week's worth of freeze-dried meals amounted to little more than five pounds?

Most, like the "lurps," were quickly disabused of the notion. They discovered that a freeze-dried dinner rated to feed two actually contained only 400 to 500 calories and so would barely feed one. They found freeze-dried entrees singularly lacking in protein (its most expensive, and therefore scarce, component). Although preparation was supposed to be as easy as adding boiling water, it wasn't so simple. Since most entrées were premixed—ham omelets, lasagna, stew, and the like—rehydrating the meat portion to palatability reduced its egg, pasta, rice, or potato portion to paste. Conversely, rehydrating the carbohydrate portion to taste left the bits of meat the consistency of croutons. Wolfing down either portion not fully rehydrated caused indigestion, gas, or heartburn, as stomach acids did the unfinished work.

ATTACK OF THE FLEXIBLE CANS

The latest militarized rations to find their way into camp, of course, are retort-packaged MREs—Meals Ready to Eat. These miracles of food packaging come in bombproof, triple-layered pouches (polyester, aluminum foil, and polypropylene). For all that high technology, in effect, they're little more than the flexible equivalent of tinned cans. The food they contain is virtually identical. Unlike dehydrated or freeze-dried foods, MREs retain their full moisture (water) content, just like canned foods. Also like canned foods, they're precooked (albeit "in the pouch" instead of the can), which affects taste and texture. Like most canned foods, they'll keep for three to five years without refrigeration.

Unlike canned foods, they're not only vitamin fortified, but also mineral and calorie fortified as well. The Department of Defense nutritionists put a lot of thought into these babies. Each MRE contains from 1,400 to 3,000 calories, so three MREs a day would fuel a hungry Clydesdale. A single serving of MRE beef stew entrée, for example, contains about 600 calories plus 70 percent of the recommended daily value (DV) of vitamin A, 24 percent of the recommended DV of vitamin C, and 34 percent of the recommended DV of iron. Compare that with a single serving of canned, commercial beef stew—which contains 300 calories, no vitamin A, 6 percent of the DV of vitamin C, and 8 percent of the DV of iron—and it's clear there is no comparison. Nowadays MREs come in more than 20 varieties, including vegetarian and ethnic entrées. For meat eaters, the options include corned beef hash, beef stew, omelet with ham, chicken and rice, and, perhaps the most popular, ham slice, or rather, "formed ham product." Vegetarians can choose from cheese tortellini, lentil stew, and pasta and vegetables. Ethnic meals include burritos, black beans and rice, and pork chow mein.

In addition to its entrée, each MRE typically includes a side dish; hard crackers; cheese spread, peanut butter, jam, or jelly; plus an accessory packet with instant coffee, nondairy creamer, sugar, salt and pepper, book matches, chewing gum, an issue of sheaved toilet paper, and a miniature bottle of Tabasco sauce—the old campaigner's standby. Each pouch also comes with an ingenious catalytic mitt: pour water into it and the resulting chemical reaction will heat the entrée scalding hot.

All these improvements carry a heavy price. Each MRE, including its abundant packaging, weighs up to 2 pounds, so three MREs a day weigh up to 6 pounds; a three-day supply can add up to a whopping 18 pounds. That's roughly the same weight as an equivalent supply of old-fashioned C-rations. What's more, they're prodigally expensive. "Civilianized" versions of MREs retail for about $6 per meal, roughly the supermarket cost of a pound of choice steak.

Despite their undoubted caloric and nutritional merits and ready-to-eat convenience, MREs taste no better than canned food in a pouch. In Somalia, troops dubbed MREs "meals rejected by Ethiopians." In the 1991 Gulf War, troops called them "meals rejected by the enemy." In the Iraq War, they've been nicknamed "meals rejected by everybody." Still, a great many hunters, anglers, and campers seek them out in surplus stores and pack them along instead of lighter, cheaper, and eminently better tasting real food.

RESURRECTING CAMP COMFORT FOOD

Unless you're going into combat or climbing K-2—where weight is a paramount consideration and you'll be out for weeks—there is absolutely no justifiable reason to forgo good eating in favor of canned, freeze-dried, or retort-packaged foods. In fact, the surest way to ruin a friendly camping trip is to pack foods more suitable for a month in the Alaska Range than a weekend in the Adirondacks.

I'm routinely horrified when a party out for a three-day camping, hunting, fishing, or backpacking trip—or even a weeklong canoeing excursion—jettisons virtually all fresh, natural foods in favor of highly processed ones. Ostensibly this is done to "lighten up" or "strip down" in preparation for the wilderness ordeal ahead. I'm politely informed that the latest developments in food engineering are lighter, last longer, travel better, and are easier to prepare than anything that's gone before. I'm admonished that fresh food's too water-heavy, perishable, fragile, and time-consuming to cook to justify taking along.

None of these explanations, pardon the pun, really holds water. In fact, they don't make practical, much less gastronomic, sense. A weekend or weeklong trip in the wilderness isn't—or at least shouldn't be—an ordeal. There's no place safer or more beautiful. Why can't outdoor adventure mean gustatory pleasure too? Why in the world, for example, take freeze-dried eggs instead of fresh? Fresh eggs will keep up to a month, without refrigeration, at moderate temperatures. Carried in their original industrially engineered containers, breakage isn't a major concern. Cracked into a skillet, they're ready to eat in a fraction of the time it takes to reconstitute and cook powdered eggs. Why take some kind of "cheese product" when natural, low-moisture cheeses like Parmesan, provolone, or Cheddar will keep just as well and taste twice—make that ten times—better? Why on earth ditch fresh potatoes for instant, when the former will keep quite well for months and you'll be out for a weekend? Why pack a single serving of MRE precooked spaghetti when, for the same weight and a fraction of the expense, you could take uncooked pasta that in a few minutes could feed four?

PART II

Back to Basics

★ CHAPTER 3 ★

BACK TO GOOD EATING

Making Meals Equal to the Outdoor Experience

Next time out, I'm going back to beans and bacon, prunes, rice—
macaroni, too. I've had enough for a lifetime of freeze-dried
chunk chicken and freeze-dried beef almondine.

—JOHN MCPHEE, 1975

ORTUNATELY FOR camp cooks, an astonishing
variety of fresh and naturally preserved foods
keep very well without refrigeration or modern
processing of any kind. Many, in fact, will travel better and
last longer in the bush than you. Their flavor, texture, and
nutritive value are so superior to their processed equivalents—whether canned, dehydrated, or freeze-dried—and
their cost so much less, that it's a culinary crime to leave
them behind. In limited quantities, on backpacking trips,
they're gustatorily worth their weight in gold.

Unfortunately, multitudes of modern-minded campers do
leave them behind. They're so starstruck by today's feats of

food engineering that they're blind to yesterday's. They forget that cheese is actually just ingeniously (and deliciously) preserved milk. They forget that pickled foods, like sauerkraut, were originally developed to preserve green vegetables (and their vitamins) through the winter. They forget that cellars were first dug not for house foundations, but for long-term storage of vegetables, fruits, and especially wine. They forget that winter squashes got their name because they actually do keep fresh all winter long. They forget that world-class gourmet foods—like dry-cured Spanish serrano, Italian prosciutto, and Virginia's Smithfield hams, or smoked sturgeon and whitefish—are really just elegant, old-fashioned solutions for keeping fresh meat and fish from going bad.

Most such naturally long-lasting foods have been forgotten for one simple reason. In our Age of Refrigeration, there's no compelling reason to remember them—at home anyway. An average-size refrigerator has a capacity of 18.5 cubic feet, roughly two-thirds of it cold storage space and one-third freezer space. Put another way: it will accommodate more than 80 pounds of fresh food and 45 pounds of frozen food—a month's worth of fresh food for a family of four. Virtually nothing need be left out of the cold.

Cold Wars

In most rustic hunting, fishing, and vacation camps, however, refrigeration's usually limited to propane-powered mini fridges. For the sake of fuel efficiency, these generally have less than half (sometimes much less) the capacity of electrically powered household models. Indeed, a typical propane mini refrigerator will store only about seven cubic feet of food supplies. Cramming one to subsist a party of four exclusively on fresh or frozen foods for two weeks is an impossibility. A week's worth is a stretch. Five days is a more realistic estimate.

On a car camping or canoe trip—lacking even a diminutive propane fridge—the cold storage shortage becomes positively Draconian. A well-insulated camp cooler will keep block ice (block, mind you, *not* cubes) frozen for about four or five days maximum in hot weather. That's if you're disciplined about keeping the lid shut at all times and quick at grabbing what you need in the brief moments when it's open. It will keep perishable foods tolerably, if sloppily, until the ice melts. But it won't accommodate much. A standard camp cooler has a capacity of 34 quarts (8.5 gallons), which sounds quite capacious (and is probably why manufacturers of coolers cite their quart, instead of cubic foot, capacity). In actuality, a 34-quart cooler contains less than 1.5 cubic feet of storage space. Compared to your home fridge (18.5 cubic feet) or camp propane mini fridge (7 cubic feet), that's Lilliputian. When you consider that a good portion of that small space must be filled with a large block of ice for the cooler to work at all, it's even tinier. That precious cold storage space is best reserved for keeping meat, fish, milk, and other food poisoning–prone items safe to eat.

On backpacking or canoe trips without coolers or ice, of course, there's no cold storage problem because there's no cold storage. Counterintuitively, that makes a camp cook's life a lot easier. There's no ice to worry about, no meltwater to drain, no foods to rotate or thaw. You can still safely pack must-refrigerate items, like fresh meat, for first-night use. Just double-wrap meat in plastic wrap and aluminum foil, then seal it in a zip-lock bag and stick it in the freezer at home overnight. Hard frozen, bundled in something insulating (a wool sweater works well), and stowed in the center of your pack, it will keep quite well for a day (perhaps two, if sunk in cold stream or lake water). Beyond that, whatever fresh foods you take had better be able to take care of themselves.

Fresh Foods Without Refrigeration

Not to worry. Fresh foods aren't nearly as perishable as you might think. Our forefathers routinely kept fruits, vegetables, cheeses, and meats fresh—in springhouses, root cellars, and smokehouses—for months. On camping trips today, which typically last from three days to a maximum of two weeks, there's really no need to refrigerate any of the following fresh foods. Handled with a modicum of care, kept shaded and open to air, they'll keep safely as long as indicated and usually longer. They will make fresh meals—not processed, packaged ones—the centerpiece of camp.

FOODS THAT WILL KEEP THREE TO FOUR WEEKS

Potatoes: It may surprise you to learn that the "fresh" potatoes sold in your local supermarket—especially the ubiquitous Idaho russet, with its cardboard box–like skin—may have been stored for up to a year. So-called new potatoes (thinner-skinned varieties like whites, reds, and golds) in your produce section may have been stored two to three months. This doesn't diminish them materially. Indeed, the fact that potatoes keep so well for so long is among the primary reasons they're so plentiful and cheap.

A five-pound sack of potatoes (about 16 medium-sized potatoes: see the "Poundwise Guide" on page 69), of any variety you like, will easily keep for up to a month. Certainly long enough to last for the duration of any camping trip you're likely to take. Just keep them in the dark and as well ventilated as you can manage. Denied light and heat, they likely won't sprout. Ventilated, they won't rot. And if there's one vegetable you want in camp, it's potatoes.

Sweet potatoes: Typically, after picking, sweet potatoes are left to cure for about two weeks before they're even marketed. It develops their natural sugars and flavor. Stored like other potatoes and kept at moderate temperature (above 50°F), they'll be good for several weeks. They are great favorites in camp when used as an alternative to potatoes.

Onions: Stored in a mesh bag or shallow, open box in a shaded, airy nook, onions will keep famously: up to two months, in fact. Even if a few chance to sprout, sending up long, green shoots, for godssakes don't throw them out: the new-grown shoots are quite good themselves. Sweet Bermuda (white), Spanish (yellow), and Italian (red) onions are famous camp keepers. Don't worry if you can't use a big one all at once. A cut onion, secured in a plastic baggie, will keep three to four days in most conditions.

Carrots: Like other root vegetables, carrots were regularly cellared all winter by pioneers and homesteaders. Oddly, few campers (children at heart) seem to like carrots by themselves. They will steadfastly refuse to eat them, however well cooked. (There is to this day, I'm certain, a bowl of the best damned sliced, buttered carrots ever made, still sitting uneaten at McQuat Lake outpost in Ontario.) Grated carrots, on the other hand, stirred into stews and soups, or sprinkled atop baked potatoes, greens, and salads, are relished and never refused. They add great taste and texture to a number of camp dishes and act as a natural thickener besides.

Parsnips: Sometimes called "white carrots," parsnips will not only keep all winter long, they'll get better. Freezing temperatures improve their naturally sweet flavor. Other than winter squash (see that entry), parsnips are probably the longest-keeping fresh vegetable there is.

Cabbage: Anything green is welcome in the wild, which is why pioneers prized the lowly, long-lasting cabbage. Green cabbage, crinkly leafed Savoy, and colorful red cabbage were regularly stored all winter. With a modicum of care, they'll easily keep on your summer camping trip. Indeed, on any trip without refrigeration, cabbage is the green standby for making salads and slaws.

Turnips and rutabagas: Related to the cabbage family, they're similarly long keepers.

Winter squash: Thick-skinned, so-called winter squashes—including acorn, buttercup, butternut, spaghetti, turban, and the massive Hubbard—were safely cellared for as long as six months in the old days. Campers today seldom consider packing them. That's a great mistake: spit-roasted, baked, boiled, mashed, and fried squash are classic American camp foods.

Garlic: Kept dry, it will remain very happy and flavorful for a long time. A few big bulbs weigh next to nothing and improve whatever they are added to immeasurably. Indeed, garlic is the camp cook's all-purpose, not-so-secret weapon. The mere scent of it alerts everyone in camp that there's some real cooking going on. Only so long as the garlic lasts, will the cook's repute: so use lavishly. You can't go wrong.

But there are reasons beyond good cooking to take fresh garlic along. The juice in garlic contains a very powerful antiseptic: squeezed and diluted with water, it can be used to treat cuts, abrasions, and bug bites. The juice also contains a natural antibiotic, useful in treating colds and infections. Medical studies suggest garlic may even help prevent cancer.

Despite all the natural goodness of old-fashioned, fresh garlic, some campers insist on substituting processed garlic powder or garlic salt in its place, in the belief the latter are somehow more concentrated or longer lasting. They aren't. Make no mistake: there is no substitute for the real article.

Radishes: Without refrigeration, radishes will remain fresh and crisp for weeks. They're especially suited for taking on backpacking trips as they're compact, stand up well to rough handling, and—like carrots—add a welcome, fresh crunch to many dishes.

Milk: I've never met a soul in the outdoors who professed a liking, much less preference, for powdered milk. Old-fashioned evaporated milk in tins, though processed, still works in the woods. But nowadays, thanks to one of the genuine advances in food technology, you can take real whole milk. Unrefrigerated Grade A, UHT (Ultra High Temperature) homogenized milk—packaged in ultratough, flexible, aseptic cartons—will keep fresh for up to six months. After opening, however, they must be refrigerated. This presents no real problem, since eight-ounce cartons are ideal for individual use or cooking purposes.

Meat and fish: For the uncool camp cook (those lacking or limited in refrigeration), keeping fresh meat and fish is usually the biggest provisioning problem. By technical definition, none of the following can really be termed fresh. All have undergone some preservation process, albeit natural, old-fashioned, time-honored ones. The old-fashioned "cures," however, render these products as long-lasting and better tasting than any of their modern equivalents.

Country-cured ham, dry cured in salt, smoked, and aged from three months to as long as a year, keeps practically indefinitely. Rid of most of its water content, it's essentially concentrated ham, so a little goes a long way; combined with its versatility, that makes it ideal for camp use (see Chapter

8, "Meat Matters"). Dried (jerked) beef, fish, or poultry (see pages 168–70) are all lightweight, keep well for months, and, reconstituted with water, plump up near to their original texture and taste. Hard salamis and other cured sausages, though heavier than dried meats, are long-lasting, perennial camp favorites. Slab bacon, sometimes called side bacon, smoked with the rind left on, will keep for months.

For those wedded to convenience, today's retort-packaged chicken, tuna, and salmon (crabmeat and clams, too) are precooked and will keep unopened for three years. Nutritionally, they are practically identical to canned chicken and seafood, but *sans* the can, they're about one-third the weight and great for backpacking. The downside is that they cost 40 to 50 percent more than their canned equivalents.

FOODS THAT WILL KEEP TWO TO THREE WEEKS

Apples: In the old days, apples were routinely cellared for months. Fresh ones will travel hardily for weeks. Good eaten whole for a healthy snack, the camp cook can also employ them baked or stewed with sugar for desserts, enfolded in flour for pies or fritters, mashed into sauce for a side dish, or sautéed with fish.

Oranges/lemons/limes: The only fruits that Thoreau took on his long canoe trips in the Maine woods were lemons. He advised taking a half-dozen on two weeklong treks to "correct the pork and warm water." They're infinitely better on fresh fish. Or to "correct" gin.

Eggs: Counterintuitively, fresh eggs are neither particularly fragile nor perishable. In fact, they're the equivalent of nature-designed MREs. Eggs are triple-protected by a solid outer shell, tough outer shell membrane, and rubbery inner shell membrane (with a very effective shock-absorbing air space between the latter two). As if that's not enough, today's supermarket eggs are coated with pharmaceutical-grade mineral oil and packaged in bombproof foam plastic cartons. The end result is an egg that will keep safely, without refrigeration, for up to a month at moderate temperatures. If backpacking or canoeing, there's no need to buy one of those special egg carriers sold in outdoor stores; their original containers work just as well. If you're packing only a half-dozen eggs, just cut the original container in half.

Store eggs separately from other foods, however. The otherwise tough shells are actually quite porous (containing up to 17,000 tiny pores per egg, to allow its precious contents to breathe). That means they'll absorb the taste and smell of anything they're packed with.

Remember, whenever using eggs, cook thoroughly (until the whites and yolk are firm).

Cheese: Experienced alpinists, backpackers, canoe trekkers, and campers always make a place for cheese in their packs: the right kind of cheese, that is. Low-moisture cheeses with a water content of about 35 percent—notably Cheddar, Monterey Jack, Parmesan, and provolone—keep and travel well in the wild. High-moisture cheeses with a water content of almost 60 percent—like Camembert and Brie—don't.

Wax-sealed cheeses will keep for several weeks. If not wax-sealed, wrap cheese in paper towels dampened with white vinegar and place in an airtight container.

Whatever you do, don't skimp on, much less forget, cheese. A big wedge of hard cheese (the bigger, the better) is as indispensable to a camp cook in the wild as garlic. It makes a perfect, no-cook ploughman's lunch (cheese and bread) while trekking or fishing, and grated or melted—into or over almost every food known to man—it creates a memorable dish.

FOODS THAT WILL KEEP UP TO ONE WEEK

Celery: Celery was routinely cold-cellared in the old days for months. If not kept in a cool, dark place, it may turn flaccid and lose moisture. But chopped up and added to soups or stews, it rehydrates to its crunchy self.

Cucumbers: Cukes will easily keep unrefrigerated for three to four days.

Bell peppers: Both green and red varieties will be good for three days unrefrigerated.

Iceberg lettuce: Unrefrigerated, iceberg will keep for three to four days, but a party of two will likely have devoured it before then.

Melons/cantaloupes: Purchased slightly unripe, small melons and cantaloupes will travel quite well and be ready to eat after three to four days.

Smoked link sausage: Smoked sausage will keep safely for a week, even in hot weather.

Summer squash: White, yellow, and zucchini squash are sweetest when they're young. Unrefrigerated, they'll be delicious for three days.

Tortillas and bagels: Tortillas will keep a week, primarily because they contain about three times as much salt as loaf bread. Bagels, dough that's been boiled and baked, and typically contains no additives, will keep up to two.

FRESH FOOD HANDLING TIPS

Don't wash fresh fruits or vegetables before packing them; it will accelerate spoilage. Likewise, don't suffocate them in plastic wrap or aluminum foil. It will do the same thing. Pack them to camp in a mesh bag, burlap sack, brown paper bag, or other breathable material. In camp, store them in a cool, shady corner, not on a windowsill. Heat and light will destroy, not ripen, them.

The same goes for eggs and cheese. After some time, cheese may show a little mold, but that's its birthright and harmless. Just scrape it off with a knife. On hot summer days, cheese may turn rubbery, but don't worry about it. Just set it in cool stream or lake water and it will revive handsomely.

FRESHFOODAPHOBIA

Despite the fact that this cornucopia of fresh food keeps naturally, without refrigeration, it's usually left at home anyway. Campers, quite wrongly, believe fresh food takes too much time and fuel to prepare or that it's simply too heavy to hump around the bush. This irrational, largely groundless fear—which an accomplished camp cook acquaintance of mine calls freshfoodaphobia—grips inexperienced and experienced outdoorspeople alike. Though they're of two disparate camps—campers out for a long weekend and hunters, anglers, and canoeists out for a week—together they account for approximately 90 percent of all camping trips taken by Americans annually. Both fall into very different, but equally grim and expensive, food traps.

THE CONVENIENCE TRAP

Roughly one-third of U.S. families go on at least one camping trip a year. Statistically, the "typical" family camping trip consists of Dad, Mom, Sis, and Junior, out for an overnight.

Pressed for time, they usually stock up on convenience foods: soft drinks, bread, sandwich makings, crackers and chips, instant soup, hot dogs, candy bars, and cookies. These seem to be foods tailor-made for a picnic in the wild. Except for the meats and drinks, none require any refrigeration. None require much (if any) preparation or cooking time. In fact, they constitute a culinary and nutritional horror story.

After a brief hike to the campsite—which in the overwhelming majority of family camping trips is considerably less than one mile—they eat a lunch fit for lumberjacks. Each camper gets a processed tuna salad sandwich on wheat bread, which seems healthy enough. In fact, it contains 417 calories, 30 percent of the recommended daily value (DV) of fat and 42 percent of the recommended DV of sodium. This is accompanied by a packet of cheese crackers (six per packet), one 12-ounce can of Coca-Cola and one 2-ounce Snickers candy bar apiece. These add another 610 calories to everyone's lunch, plus 24 percent more of the recommended DV of fat and 30 percent more of the recommended DV of salt.

Supper's equally trouble-free to prepare and, to outward appearances, equally innocuous. Every camper gets a cup of instant chicken noodle soup, potato chips, two grilled hot dogs (on a bun with mustard or ketchup), another can of Coke, and two big chocolate cookies for dessert. These add another whopping 2,272 calories to everybody's diet, along with 165 percent of the recommended DV of fat and 173 percent of the recommended DV of sodium.

The end result is a nutritionist's nightmare. In just two meals, Dad, Mom, Sis, and Junior have each consumed nearly 3,300 calories apiece, far beyond what they require for a lazy walk in the woods. In addition, they've eaten twice as much fat and more than twice as much sodium as is good for them. Calorically, everybody's overfed. Gustatorily, nobody's particularly happy. Beyond the fleeting warmth of a cup of soup and two charred hot dogs, there's been no hot meal. All the salt's left everybody thirsty. By dark, when the forest turns chill, everyone retires gloomily to the tent.

Real Convenience Food

If you've got to go the convenience camper route—and most people do for some outings—stop at your local supermarket, not 7–Eleven. It'll be just as quick, less expensive, and much better eating.

Instead of canned soft drinks, pick up some good old Kool-Aid. It's been around since 1927 and for good reason. One 0.23-ounce packet (roughly one-fiftieth the weight of one can of Coke) will make 64 ounces (equivalent to more than five cans of Coke) of whatever flavor you like. What's more, it's orders of magnitude cheaper and lighter to carry to camp. Unlike Coke, Kool-Aid is sodium-free and each 8-ounce glass contains 10 percent of the DV of vitamin C, so you can feel saintly about serving it up to your camp mates.

For lunch, instead of processed sandwich spreads heavy with mayonnaise, pick up some fresh-cut lunch meat (turkey or lean roast beef) and serve on wheat bread with hot mustard. It'll be higher in protein and fiber and much lower in fat and sodium. Forgo the candy bars and instead take fresh apples, oranges, or raisins, all of which are fat- and salt-free.

For a healthier, effortless, and truly satisfying hot meal for supper, ditch the instant soup and hot dogs. Go back to the venerable official Boy Scout manual and make tried-and-true "hobos" (glorified as "hamburger à la foil" in the manual's latest edition). Buy a pound of lean ground beef, four medium potatoes, four small white onions, four carrots, and eight ears of sweet corn. In aggregate, the weight of these fresh foods will be about equal to the 12-pack of Coke you've sensibly left behind. Besides being good and quick, the preparation of these fresh ingredients will give every camper (especially kids) something involving and "outdoorsy" to do. What's more, since everything's cooked in aluminum foil, there are no pots or dishes for adults to wash afterward.

Each camper forms a quarter pound of ground beef (which contains quite as many calories, more protein, yet 30 percent less fat and considerably less salt than two hot dogs) into a patty; slices one potato, one onion, and one carrot into pieces (the fresh vegetables are carbohydrate- and vitamin-rich, but fat- and sodium-free); and wraps all the ingredients in heavy-duty aluminum foil. The crimped foil package is then set on hot coals for 15 minutes. While it's cooking, everyone shucks two ears of fresh corn, seals them tightly in aluminum foil, and sets them on the coals alongside the main course for 10 minutes.

In little more than a half hour, everybody's wolfing down his or her own hot and personally cooked supper, which makes it twice as good. For dessert—stowed in the soft drink–free cooler—are fresh, sweet watermelon wedges. Afterward, as the woods turn chill, the cooking coals are brought to a bright, cheery blaze with more wood. Over the fire, campers roast marshmallows (24 calories apiece) on sticks. There's no need to worry how many of these the kids eat: they're fat- and sodium-free, and few kids can eat the 12 to 18 that equal the calories in a single candy bar or big chocolate cookie. As the fire burns down, a pot of water is brought to boil to make everyone an eight-ounce mug of instant cocoa before bedtime. If Dad's smart, he'll leaven his and Mom's with a jigger (1.5 ounces) of brandy or rum. Filled with hot food and sipping hot chocolate, everyone wonders at the myriad stars suddenly visible overhead. Before Dad can douse the coals and make his way to the tent, everybody else is inside, zipped into sleeping bags and asleep.

THE WEIGHT TRAP

The weight of provisions is the biggest bugaboo and nonissue in the whole realm of camping. It's the principal reason most campers eat miserably, instead of handsomely. And there's no reason for it.

It's estimated that somewhat less than 10 percent of campers in the U.S. makes a weeklong trek in the wild annually. Most of those who do base themselves in a deer shack, fishing camp, or public campground where access by auto, boat, or floatplane renders weight and provisioning concerns pretty much moot. Or they book trips where outfitters, packers, or guides are paid to make all weighty provisioning and cooking problems go away.

The minority who truly venture off on their own—by backpack or canoe—are wonderfully free of everything but their stomachs. As human beings are quite rightly described as "eating machines," however, this poses an immediate, unending obstacle—how far and long the human engine can range on a fixed quantity of food, or more properly, fuel. Since most human beings, given half a chance, are notoriously lazy, they choose foods they think are the easiest to prepare or lightest to carry. Those criteria can lead to dismal eating in the wild.

According to the renowned wilderness experts at the National Outdoor Leadership Schools (NOLS), an adult engaged in "average wilderness activities"—active backpacking, canoeing, ski touring, and so on—requires from 2,500 to 3,000 calories a day or, more practically put, 1.5 to 2 pounds of food daily. Those calories (energy) must necessarily come from proteins (about 1,800 calories/pound), carbohydrates (also about 1,800 calories/pound), and fats (about 4,100 calories/pound). Nutritionally, adults require a balance of all three. Generally, as a percentage of total calories, it's recommended that 20 percent be supplied by protein (beef, chicken, fish, beans, lentils, cheese, peanut butter), 20 percent by fat (oils, butter, whole milk, nuts, chocolate, and animal fats in beef, pork, lamb, poultry, and fish), and 60 percent by carbohydrates (breads, fruits, potatoes, pasta, rice, vegetables, oatmeal). In provisioning for an extended trip in the wild, those criteria are paramount. Food composition and calories per pound—not convenience or lightness—are what matter.

For trekkers travelling by canoe, weight is not really as much a consideration as it may first appear. A 16-foot aluminum canoe (weighing about 60 pounds), for instance, can easily carry a load of 1,000 pounds, including paddlers. Assuming two portly (225-pound) paddlers, that allows 550 pounds of cargo. If half is devoted to camp equipment (tent, sleeping bags, cook kit, aid kit, stove/fuel, axe/saw, personal duffel) and the remaining half devoted to provisions, two canoeists can easily embark enough food (at two pounds per person per day) for 68 days. As a practical matter, however, canoe trips that long are exceptional. Most canoe trips last an average of 7 to 10 days. For that length of time, you're better off—financially and gustatorily—packing an old-fashioned combination of unadulterated fresh or dried foods and naturally preserved meat than their canned or freeze-dried counterparts. Hauling the admittedly heavier former options over portages, depending on terrain, weather, and bugs, of course, can be a hardship, but a temporary one. And the reward of eating well at the end of the day will erase all trials from the mind.

For backpackers, however, the trial's a more or less unending one. Every ounce must be carried day in and day out. According to the venerable Mountaineers organization (based in Seattle, Washington), the traditional limit for a backpacking trek—on which hikers carry all their own provisions, without a resupply—is 14 days maximum. Based upon experience, that makes a helluva heavy load, even packing ultralight, precooked, packaged foods. Gustatorially it amounts to eating a mountain of powdered eggs, powdered milk, instant oatmeal, instant rice, instant potatoes, instant soup, and freeze-dried entrées. Two weeks of it is a dietary ordeal few who have endured it wish to repeat. In fact, in more than 40 years of backpacking, I can count—on somewhat less than the fingers of two hands—the number of acquaintances who've fed for two weeks out of a rucksack alone. All of them were either alpinists marooned by foul weather or long-trail hikers consumed with logging miles. For both it was misery.

Statistically, the overwhelming majority of backpackers don't venture into the wild for two weeks or even one. An estimated 80 percent make trips lasting a maximum of three days. In most cases, the average party size is two adults, usually male. Despite the brief duration, however (or perhaps because of the abundant testosterone involved), they typically provision as if they were through-hiking from Georgia to Maine. They put on their hair shirts and leave everything but freeze-dried foods behind.

This appears to make perfect sense. From the freeze-dried rack at their local camping store, they happily select three featherweight breakfasts, three dinner entrées, assorted vegetables for side dishes, and three kinds of trail snacks. In aggregate, all this food (three days' worth) weighs only $3\frac{1}{4}$ pounds in 16 compact, bombproof pouches. It's shockingly expensive—over $80 ($83.75 to be exact)—but seemingly money well worth spent. No meal takes longer than ten minutes to cook. Indeed, other than adding a cup or two of boiling water and stirring, no cooking's involved. Every meal can be prepared and eaten in its plastic packaging, so there are no dishes to wash. Each package is rated to provide two full servings. It seems the ultralight, ultraconvenient answer to a backpacker's prayer.

On the trail, the food appears very different. The first morning's breakfast consists of a 3.5-ounce pouch of freeze-dried scrambled eggs (440 calories for two) and two 1.5-ounce pouches of freeze-dried sausage patties (220 calories/pouch), reconstituted with boiling water and left to sit for ten minutes. It is not a success. Each camper gets a lukewarm cup of soggy eggs and two rubbery, credit card–sized sausage patties, providing each fellow a spartan allowance of 440 calories, roughly equivalent to a dieter's breakfast at home. It is not enough to jump-start the day. Still hungry, they proceed to devour the next day's breakfast: a 9.5-ounce pouch of granola cereal with blueberries (530 calories). It is something of a race between them to the bottom of the pouch. The granola fills them up, but doesn't adequately feed them. In all, the men have consumed 705 calories each, enough to break camp and start them on their way, but less than a quarter of their daily requirement for wilderness trekking. The fact that the breakfast(s) they've just eaten cost $21.25 darkens an otherwise splendid morning.

At midday, after four hours of hiking and burning 540 calories apiece (a 170-pound man carrying a 30-pound pack burns about 135 calories/hour), they eat a snack of freeze-dried fudge brownies. They're good—hard to distinguish from fresh, in fact. The only problem is there aren't enough. The four-ounce pouch (420 calories net), shared equally (210 calories apiece), hardly quiets their rumbling stomachs. By unanimous vote, they rip open another freeze-dried snack, a four-ounce pouch of bananas Foster. It's heartier than the brownies (500 calories net), yet wolfed down just as quickly. Unsurprisingly, they're still hungry. Each man's share of midday snacks amounts to 460 calories: barely enough to refuel them for the remainder of the day.

Four hours later, footsore and ravenous, having burned another 540 calories apiece, they make camp. In pitching the tent, gathering wood, hauling water, and other chores, they each burn another 100 calories apiece, keenly anticipating dinner. It appears more promising than breakfast, from the looks of the label anyway. This meal consists of a four-ounce pouch of freeze-dried beef stew, with a banner that says, "Makes 20 full ounces! Dinner for two." Closer examination of the package, however, reveals it isn't beef stew, but "stew with beef," which is the difference between a steer and its moo. Of the 13 listed ingredients, only one is beef. Three are vegetables: potatoes, green peas (freeze-dried), and carrots (dehydrated, not freeze-dried). The remaining ten ingredients are beef broth seasoning (sans any trace of beef), cornstarch (a thickener), vegetable flavor (corn syrup, sugar, soy sauce), onion powder (not onions, mind you), salt, cream powder (a binder), butter powder (nonfat milk and more salt), corn oil, and spices (apparently too mundane to merit individual mention). Reconstituted with boiling water in its own plastic bag, the stew does indeed quintuple in size to an impressive 20 ounces. Divided equally by firelight, however, it is less than impressive. Each ravenous camper gets $1^1/4$ cups, containing a parsimonious 225 calories. By comparison, the 460 calories of snacks each fellow had at noon was a feast.

What follows hardly requires explanation. The next day's dinner (also rated to serve two)—a 5-ounce pouch of freeze-dried chicken teriyaki with rice (560 calories net or 280 calories/man)—is quickly reconstituted with boiling water and eaten. So are all the freeze-dried vegetable side dishes (three 1.5-ounce pouches of peas, corn, and mixed vegetables, respectively), which together add another 240 calories to each

man's plate. In chowing down all this freeze-dried food—
which has taken a good hour, not ten minutes, to prepare in
sequence—each camper's allowance amounts to 745 calories.

They both go to bed feeling hungry and totally unsatisfied.
This is understandable. In the course of the day, each man
has burned 3,050 calories (1,870 fuelling his basal metabo-
lism and another 1,180 humping in the bush). Each man's in-
take of freeze-dried foods, on the other hand, totals a miserly
1,910 calories—a third less than required.

The next morning, the remaining freeze-dried breakfast
and dinner will be wolfed down to fuel a hasty retreat back
to the trailhead and car, where an equally hasty drive will de-
liver the campers to the nearest fast-food outlet to gorge.

A BETTER WEIGH

There is no need for such nonsense. On a three-day backpack
outing—which is the norm—you can take pretty much
whatever foods you like. True, the fresh, good stuff will weigh
roughly three to four times more than freeze-dried. In practical terms, though, on a three-day outing for two, the net difference between the two amounts to somewhat less than 7
pounds (6 3/4 pounds).

I don't know about you, but I'll quite happily hump my
3-pounds-plus share of that to eat wonderfully—instead of
woefully—in the wild.

I'll forgo taking 8 ounces of expensive freeze-dried eggs,
sausage, and cereal to feed two people a lukewarm, flaccid
breakfast of 600 calories apiece. I'd rather substitute 12
ounces of cheaper, better-tasting fresh food—four fresh eggs,
six slices of bacon, and four English muffins—to feed two
adults a hot, bracing breakfast of 850 calories each.

I'll skip the 8 ounces of freeze-dried snacks that give each
hiker 540 calories apiece. I'd rather substitute 12 ounces of

time-tested, more satisfying staples—like Parmesan, hard salami, and dry roasted peanuts—that will give them 740 calories each.

I'll leave on the shelf the astronomically priced 4-ounce pouches of freeze-dried dinner entrées, advertised to feed two, but containing less than 250 calories per person. Eight ounces of pasta (50 cents' worth), with 1.5 ounces of dried tomato or pesto mix and 1 ounce of grated cheese, will satisfy each camper more than twice as well (almost 600 calories apiece) and take little more time to prepare. Eight ounces of homemade beef jerky (see page 168) with two fresh potatoes, chopped onion, and fresh-made flour dumplings (see page 156) will do likewise. Twelve ounces of fresh sausage with 10 ounces of raw (real) rice will take twice as long to make as a freeze-dried dinner (20 vs. 10 minutes), but will feed each camper far, far better (1,200 calories vs. 250).

In fact, for a three-day backpacking trip—if you want to eat well—leave the freeze-dried food, not the fresh, at home. For a party of two, you'll fare far better gustatorily to fill your pack instead with 10 to 12 pounds of good, natural stuff, like the preceding (see Chapter 4, "The Grub List"). Naturally (and I use the word reverently), these foods eclipse the weight of any freeze-dried equivalents. On the other hand, the fresh stuff contains 14,500 calories, while the freeze-dried equivalents contain less than 6,000. That, of course, is the difference between a complaining stomach and a satisfied one.

Expense-wise, the gap between the two is wider than the Grand Canyon. In aggregate, the good, fresh, or naturally preserved foods just listed cost about $30, or about $0.23 per ounce. Their freeze-dried counterparts retail for a total of about $84, an average of roughly $1.75 per ounce. Indeed, the cost per ounce of many freeze-dried items is far higher than that. A 1.55-ounce packet of freeze-dried pork sausage patties (one serving, containing 220 calories) retails for $5.50—a sticker-shocking $3.55 per ounce. A 0.42-ounce packet of freeze-dried green beans (two servings, each containing 25 calories) retails for $3—a mind-boggling $7.14 per ounce.

To put those prices in perspective, USDA Choice New York strip steak from your local supermarket costs about $0.50 per ounce. A whole, precooked Maine lobster, from a specialty food retailer, shipped overnight to your home, costs $2.35 an ounce, premium rack of lamb $2.90 an ounce.

If better taste and higher calorie count don't tempt you back to the basics of good eating in the outdoors, cost alone should.

CHAPTER 4

THE GRUB LIST

150 Years of Advice on Provisioning for the Wild

Don't forget nothing.

—MAJOR ROBERT ROGERS, "STANDING ORDERS," 1759

COMPOSING THE dog-eared, smudged grub list is, by far, the camp cook's most challenging—and daunting—task. Food, after all, largely determines the success—or failure—of any outdoor trip. As an outfitter once told me: "There's nothing else folks can complain about three times a day."

They will. Let them. It's camp tradition and all in good fun (well, reasonably fun). And it's unavoidable. Given all the variables a camp cook has to juggle—size of party, mode of travel, duration and difficulty of trip, weather, availability of fuel and water, means of cooking, preparation time, personal preferences and prejudices—the probability of composing a grub list that accommodates everybody is a virtual impossibility. It's useless, really, to try. Deft attention must be paid, however, to making absolutely certain of two things. One: that there's enough food for all (no one ever complains about second helpings). And two: that it cannot only be made simply, but more important, made well.

The basic logistics of provisioning aren't hard. Figuring $1^{1}/2$ to 2 pounds of food per day per adult, you can't go far wrong (calorically anyway). The hard part's choosing foods that in variety, quality, and simplicity combine to truly satisfy. Camp cooks are well advised to remember that—contrary to popular opinion—Napoleon never said, "An army marches on its stomach." He said, "Soup makes the soldier." Anyone who enjoys eating well in the outdoors knows the difference. It doesn't just take food; it takes good food, the kind that not only fills bellies but also warms hearts and elevates spirits. Eating well in the field also requires a calculated assortment of foods that, prepared alone or in concert, provide the cook the greatest culinary range, but not too much to pack or portage.

That makes one piece of equipment—the grub list—critical to the success of any camping, hunting, or fishing trip. To begin building a great one of your own, check out these provisioning lists from the past. Thoreau, Nessmuk, Hemingway, Sigurd Olson, L. L. Bean, and John McPhee can teach you a lot.

Thoreau's List, 1846

"Simplify" was Thoreau's principle in provisioning as well as in life. His grub list for "an excursion of 12 days into the Maine woods with a companion and one Indian" was about as simple as it gets. It consisted of 28 pounds of ship's bread (hardtack), 16 pounds of salt pork, 12 pounds of sugar, 3 pounds of coffee, 3 pounds of rice, 1 quart of Indian (corn) meal, 1 pint of salt, and 6 lemons.

Thoreau wrote that he was perfectly content eating "a

piece of ship's bread in one hand and a piece of fried pork in the other"—for breakfast, lunch, and dinner. It's doubtful his companions were. This amounted to a rather spartan allowance of about $1\frac{1}{4}$ pounds of food per man per day, just enough to remind a fellow that paddling and portaging are hungry work. No matter how creatively prepared, it could hardly have been epicurean. Maybe the coffee kept them going: enough for four cups a day apiece, with five teaspoons of sugar in every one. They varied the monotony with fresh fish and pails of fresh-picked blueberries and raspberries.

At lumber camps along the route—by his own confession—Thoreau gorged on everything within reach. At McCauslin's camp, by his careful accounting, he wolfed down "piping hot wheaten cakes [pancakes] . . . ham, eggs, potatoes, and milk and cheese . . . and also shad and salmon, tea sweetened with molasses, and sweetcakes . . . with cranberries, stewed and sweetened, for dessert."

Lesson: so much for simplicity; the inner man craved more.

NESSMUK'S LIST, 1897

George Washington Sears, writing under the pen name "Nessmuk" for *Forest and Stream* at the turn of the nineteenth century, favored plain cooking.

For condiments, he endorsed only four: salt and cayenne pepper (premixed, in a 10-to-1 ratio, in a waterproof tin), freshly ground white pepper (never black), and lemons. He advised taking cornmeal, not flour. He thought it superior for making johnnycake (he cordially despised flour-made pancakes) and frying trout. Though he was a connoisseur of fine coffee, he didn't take it to the woods. "On a heavy knapsack and rifle tramp among the mountains, or a lone canoe cruise in a strange wilderness," he wrote, "I prefer tea." Specifically: green tea for trekking, and either black or oolong in camp.

Like Thoreau, his mainstays were hard bread and salt pork. Unlike Thoreau, he was an accomplished camp cook. Though he traveled just as light, he included dried beans and fresh onions to make soups, stews, and baked beans. He also packed fresh potatoes to pit-bake, boil, or fry.

He religiously refused to carry canned food himself. He was not, however, above greedily consuming canned goodies carried by others. "I often have a call to pilot some young, muscular friend into the deep forest," he wrote, "and he usually carries a large pack-basket with a full supply of quart cans of salmon, tomatoes, peaches, etc. I admonish him kindly, but firmly, on the folly of hauling such luxuries. But at night, when the campfire burns brightly, and he begins to fish out his tins, I make amends by allowing him to divide the groceries."

Lesson: plain fare may have been best. A few luxuries were better.

HEMINGWAY'S LIST, 1919

After his return from service as an ambulance driver with the Italian army in World War I, Hemingway headed for the North Woods. On a solo trout-fishing trip in upper Michigan, he recalled his menu in the short story "Big Two-Heart River."

Dinner the first night out was a can of pork and beans and a can of spaghetti, poured together in a skillet and brought to a simmer. Over this he poured a bottle of tomato ketchup. He sopped it up with a half loaf of store-bought bread. For dessert, he had canned apricots—"better than fresh apricots," he wrote—doubly enjoyed because he simply "liked opening cans."

Breakfast, next morning, consisted of buckwheat flapjacks,

fried in canned lard and slathered with canned apple butter. Half were chased down with coffee, sweetened with condensed milk (more cans). The rest were folded in half, wrapped in wax paper, and stuffed in his shirt pockets for a midmorning snack. Lunch—sliced raw onion sandwiches dipped in cold stream water—was an acquired taste.

Dinner, of course, consisted of three fine-sized trout: all masterfully caught, rolled in cornmeal, barded with bacon, and masterfully fried.

He was Hemingway, after all.

Lesson: "sweat equity" buys you the freedom to eat anything and everything you like—in whatever combination pleases you—so long as you can carry it.

L. L. BEAN'S LIST, 1942

Bean's recommended grub list—which he characterized as "just about right for a party of two adults for 6 or 7 days"— makes Hemingway's look anorexic. It included more than 13 pounds of bread, flour, cornmeal, oatmeal, pancake mix, cookies, and doughnuts; 8 pounds of potatoes (roughly 24 spuds); 7 pounds of meat (salt pork, bacon, and corned beef); 7 pounds of canned fruit and vegetables; a dozen eggs; 2 pounds of butter; 2 pounds of sugar; $1^{1}/4$ pounds of coffee and tea; 1 quart of syrup; $^{1}/2$ pound of salt and baking powder; plus pepper, vinegar, and mustard.

The whole list topped out at over 44 pounds of food and condiments—a whopping $3^{1}/4$ pounds of chow per man per day. That's over a pound more than what's recommended for extreme mountaineering in the Himalayas, much less a summer fishing trip in Maine.

To eat your way through Bean's grub list, every day you'd have to pack away a minimum of 10 pancakes, a bowl of oatmeal, 1 egg, 6 cups of coffee, 9 teaspoons of sugar, 7 slices of bread, 2 tablespoons of butter, 2 medium potatoes, $\frac{1}{3}$ pound of bacon or pork, a handful of cookies, and a doughnut.

Every other day—on top of that—you'd have to eat six generous servings (one serving each) of canned corned beef, canned baked beans, cornbread, canned corn, canned tomatoes, and canned peaches.

The feeding frenzy didn't stop there. Bean suggested: "If you plan to be away from camp at lunch time each day, add at least 2 loaves of bread to the above list." That's 44 slices. It's a wonder anyone had any appetite for fresh-caught fish.

Lesson: too much food can be quite as dispiriting as too little.

McPhee's List, 1975

Packing light to accommodate portages on a birchbark canoe trip retracing Thoreau's 1846 route through the Allegash country, John McPhee took freeze-dried food. It was, for its time, the latest state-of-the-art stuff available: "expensive, shining foil packets from the rugged boutiques," as he put it. The variety was alluring: freeze-dried omelets, shrimp Creole, beef stroganoff, turkey tetrazzini, beef almondine, tuna salad, chunk chicken, raspberry-apple crunch, pears, peaches, and "astronaut ice cream." It was eminently sensible: feather-light, easy to prepare, no cooking required. But it proved an outright culinary disaster.

Why? One dish was virtually indistinguishable from the next. The meat, whether shrimp, beef, tuna, or chicken, tasted like croutons. The rice or noodles accompanying it were pasty or flaccid. Everything tasted, more or less, of salt. Nothing, stirred with boiling water in its self-contained plastic bag, smelled or looked wholesome or appetizing. Indeed, McPhee found freeze-dried foods so objectionable he called them "violations of the wild." Fortunately, he'd had the foresight to tuck a collapsible reflector oven, some Crisco, and some Bisquick in his pack. With these, he delighted his fellow paddlers with fresh-baked gingerbread, drop biscuits, bannock bread, and fresh-water clams, dredged in flour and deep-fried.

Afterward he wrote: "Next time out, I'm going back to beans and bacon, prunes, rice—and macaroni, too. I have had enough for a lifetime of freeze-dried chicken and freeze-dried beef almondine. I would prefer to eat emerald [rancid green] jerky in peanut butter." McPhee returned, in a way, to where Thoreau and Nessmuk had left off.

Lesson: back to nature means back to good old-fashioned basics.

SIGURD OLSON'S TRADITIONAL AND TIMELESS LIST

Years of researching and experimenting with various old-timers' grub lists has convinced me that legendary outdoor writer/conservationist Sig Olson's is one of the best. He composed it in 1935, based on his experience as a guide in the Border Lakes canoe country between Minnesota and Ontario. By any measure, it's a masterpiece of the camp cook's art.

Calculated to feed "a canoe or camping party of two for 10 days," it consists almost entirely of fresh, whole, dried, or traditionally preserved foods. Weightwise, it amounts to about 54 pounds, or 2.55 pounds per person per day—just about ideal for average to strenuous wilderness activity. Variety-wise, it consists of about 40 individual items, all of which can be cooked deliciously, alone or in myriad combinations.

I give the list in its entirety. For eating well on canoe trips, or in no-frills fish camps and hunting shacks, you'll find nothing better.

1 pound Crisco
5 pounds bacon [salt/smoke cured, unsliced]
2 pounds ham [salt/smoke cured]
1 pound salt pork
1 pound dried beef
1 pound hard sausage
1 pound corned beef [canned]
1 dozen eggs [fresh]
1 pound cheese [low-moisture Parmesan or Cheddar]
2 pounds margarine [keeps better than butter]
7 small cans milk [evaporated]
1 pound flour
1 pound cornmeal
1 box Bisquick
3 pounds pancake flour [such as Bisquick]
1 pound oatmeal
4 loaves bread
1 pound pasta
1 pound rice
1 pound dried beans [navy]
3 pounds potatoes [about 9 medium]
1 pound onions [about 3 medium]
1 pound tomatoes [canned]
2 packages dried soup mix
1 pound raisins
3 pounds dried fruit
1$\frac{1}{4}$ pounds jam
1 pound bittersweet chocolate
2 pounds sugar [1 pound white, 1 pound brown]
1 pound salt
$\frac{1}{4}$ pound black pepper
1 pound coffee [whole bean]
$\frac{1}{4}$ pound tea

Lesson: what appears to be a boring list of long-keeping staples actually provides any halfway competent camp cook with the materials to make a great variety of memorable outdoor meals.

For breakfast, the possibilities include bacon or ham and eggs; French toast; pancakes; cheese omelets; ham, red-eye gravy, and biscuits; oatmeal and raisins; fish cakes and bannock bread; hash-brown potatoes; and plenty of fresh-ground, aromatic coffee, well leavened with milk and sugar. For quick lunches: cured sausage, cheese, hardtack with jam, hot soup, dried fruit, and chocolate. For supper: ham steaks and cornbread; pasta carbonara, fried fish with hush puppies or onion rings, beef stew with dumplings, "dirty rice," corned beef and potatoes, fish chowder, real pork and beans, real macaroni and cheese, and sautéed fish with potato pancakes. For desserts: stewed fruit with sugar, fresh baked pie or fritters, doughnuts, crêpes with fresh berries.

Three Do-It-Yourself Grub Lists

In composing your own grub list, keep the lessons of the old-timers in mind. Keep menus simple, but not too simple. A few luxuries go far. Take whatever food you like, as long as you haul it yourself. Resist the temptation, however appealing, of hauling everything you want. Old-fashioned staples add to, rather than limit, the number and variety of dishes any old camp cook can achieve.

The grub lists following will show you how to eat fresh and well, no matter what kind of camping trip you're planning. Each is based upon the *average* length of the three most common camping trips most of us take. As pounds of food per person per day is the best measure for outdoor provisioning in general, all quantities are expressed in ounces or pounds.

The "Poundwise Guide" guide at the end of this chapter will save you the time and trouble of weighing items yourself. Like all grub lists, the following are necessarily subjective and largely, if not entirely, a matter of personal taste.

BACKPACKING GRUB LIST: 2 ADULTS x 3 DAYS

Sadly, backpacking has always been the culinary Gulag of camp cooking. It needn't be. As mentioned earlier, backpackers can eat quite wonderfully and economically in the wild, as they have in the past, without resorting to today's woefully overprocessed, overpriced alternatives.

The following list totals from about 10 pounds (asterisked/ basic items) to 14 pounds (unasterisked/elective items). For a party of two, of course, that amounts to some 5 to 7 pounds for each person to carry, roughly the equivalent of a two-person tent, which is not inconsequential. Many of my backpacking colleagues, wedded to freeze-dried and/or packaged foods, rail against carrying such weight. I don't. It will provide two adults with nine genuinely satisfying meals, enough for three full, active days in the bush. In aggregate, it equals some $1^1/4$ pounds to $2^1/4$ pounds of food per person per day: just about what the National Outdoor Leadership Schools (NOLS) calculate is right to fuel a moderate to strenuous backpacking trip. Indeed, the 14-pound list may be a bit more than two can eat. But that is a good problem to have in the wild.

Meat
1 pound beef jerky* (not the wretched, expensive, store-bought stuff, but the infinitely better, cheaper, homemade variety; see page 168)
1 pound smoked bacon*
12 ounces pork sausage* (for first-night use)

3 1/2 ounces crabmeat* (real, wild-caught crabmeat, in retort pouch, at your local supermarket: one of the few modern advances worth taking to the woods)

Dairy
1 1/4 pounds cheese* (12 ounces Cheddar, 8 ounces Parmesan)
8 ounces margarine (in a plastic bottle at your local supermarket)
8 ounces milk (1 retort carton UHT milk)
6 ounces fresh eggs* (6 eggs)

Produce
10 ounces fresh potatoes* (2 medium)
10 ounces fresh apples (2 medium)
6 ounces fresh onion* (1 medium)
8 ounces fresh garlic (1 head)

Bread/Flour/Rice/Pasta
14 ounces all-purpose flour (for pancakes, biscuits, bannock, dumplings)
12 ounces English muffins* (6 muffins)
10 ounces seasoned yellow rice*
8 ounces pasta*
8 ounces cornmeal (for pancakes, biscuits, bannock, dumplings)

Snacks/Desserts
1 pound nuts* (1/4 pound each: almonds, cashews, peanuts, and pistachios)
1 pound dried fruit (1/4 pound each: apricots, bananas, pears, and raisins)
12 ounces chocolate

6 ounces jam/preserves (in a plastic screw-top container)

6 ounces peanut butter (in a plastic screw-top container)

Beverages

4 ounces freshly ground coffee (enough to make 2 to 3
strong cups per person per day)

1 ounce powdered fruit drink, such as Kool-Aid (four
$1/4$-ounce packets in various flavors; will make
8 quarts)

CANOEING GRUB LIST: 2 ADULTS x 10 DAYS

One of the memories of the first canoe trip I ever took—an
eight-day paddle in the Boundary Waters–Quetico Wilderness
made over 20 years ago—still haunts me. I'm camped on the
gin-clear waters of a long lake, sitting by a fragrant birch-
wood fire, mesmerized by a magnificent sunset and sym-
phony of loons—and eating a bowl of freeze-dried chili-mac.
Everything was perfect but the food.

It needn't happen to you. Provision yourself with fresh or
traditionally preserved fare; longer cooking, but infinitely
better eating.

Meat

$2^1/2$ pounds bacon (smoked, slab)

2 pounds country ham (steaks)

3 pounds beef jerky

3 pounds hard/dry sausage (1 pound Genoa, 1 pound
Jaeger, 1 pound chorizo)

Dairy

2 pounds cheese ($1^1/2$ pounds Cheddar, $1/2$ pound
Parmesan)

2 pounds margarine

$1\frac{1}{2}$ pounds milk (three 8-ounce retort cartons UHT milk)
1 pound fresh eggs (1 dozen)

Produce
2 pounds fresh potatoes (6 or 7 medium potatoes)
2 pounds fresh green cabbage (1 head)
2 pounds fresh onions (about 4 large)
1 pound fresh celery (1 bunch, 8 to 12 ribs)
1 pound fresh apples (about 6 medium)
1 pound fresh oranges (about 4 medium)
$\frac{1}{2}$ pound fresh lemons (about 4 medium)
8 ounces fresh garlic (1 head)

Bread/Flour/Rice/Beans/Pasta
$2\frac{1}{2}$ pounds fresh bread (2 loaves)
1 box Bisquick ($2\frac{1}{2}$ pounds)
$2\frac{1}{2}$ pounds bagels (about 20)
2 pounds cornmeal
1 pound oatmeal or grits
1 pound wild rice
1 pound dried beans (navy, Great Northern, or pinto)
1 pound pasta

Snacks/Desserts
$2\frac{1}{4}$ pounds peanut butter
2 pounds dried fruit
$1\frac{1}{4}$ pounds jam or preserves
$1\frac{1}{4}$ pounds chocolate (about six $3\frac{1}{2}$-ounce bars)
1 pound mixed nuts
1 pound dried soup mix (about eight 2-ounce packets)

Beverages
1 pound fresh whole coffee beans (see page 93.)

¹⁄₄ pound tea (about 25 tea bags)
¹⁄₄ pound cocoa

Condiments

2 pounds (about 1 quart) cooking oil (for frying fish,
   potatoes, onions, etc.)
1 pound sugar
1 pound (about 1 pint) maple syrup (leave faux,
   artificially flavored maple syrup behind and take the
   genuine article: Grade AA, dark)

CAR CAMPING/BASE CAMP GRUB LIST:
4 ADULTS x 7 DAYS

The beauty of a base camp trip is that *everybody* can go—
regardless of age, fitness level, or physical handicap. Usually
that means bigger groups and more mouths to feed, but that
needn't trouble the cook. Even though base camps vary
dramatically—from off-the-grid hunting and fishing shacks,
to state or national forest campgrounds with electricity and
water hook-ups, to fancy rental cabins with nearly all the
conveniences of home—foodwise they have two things in
common: provisions are generally driven, boated, or flown in,
and some kind of long-term cold storage—propane fridge or
ice chest—is usually available. Weight and refrigeration are
secondary concerns.

That opens up an all-new world for true camp "foodies."
The only limits are imagination and budget. The following
list consists of foods found in almost every supermarket.
They weigh a bit over 87 pounds total; heavy, to be sure, but
easily transported by car, boat, or aircraft. These provisions
will generously (gluttonously, in fact) feed a party of four for
a week, but that's the purpose of the list. Items requiring refrigeration are noted with an asterisk.

Meat

3 pounds fresh chicken (about 1 whole chicken)*

$2^{1}/_{2}$ pounds bacon (smoked, slab)

2 pounds beef steak (four 8-ounce filets)*

2 pounds country ham (steaks)

2 pounds hard/dry sausage

$1^{1}/_{2}$ pounds stew beef*

1 pound pork chops*

1 pound fresh pork sausage*

Dairy

4 pounds milk (2 quarts)*

3 pounds cheese (1 pound Cheddar, 1 pound Monterey
   Jack, 1 pound Parmesan)

2 pounds fresh eggs (2 dozen)

2 pounds butter*

$^{1}/_{2}$ pound cream cheese*

Produce

3 pounds lettuce and cabbage (2 heads iceberg lettuce,
   1 head green cabbage)

$2^{3}/_{4}$ pounds potatoes (about 8 large)

$2^{1}/_{2}$ pounds yellow squash (about 4 medium)

2 pounds acorn squash (about 4 small)

2 pounds sweet potatoes (about 4 large)

2 pounds onions (about 4 large)

2 pounds fresh corn (8 ears)

1 pound carrots (about 10 medium)

$1^{1}/_{2}$ pounds apples (about 8)

$1^{1}/_{2}$ pounds oranges (about 8)

$1^{1}/_{2}$ pounds cantaloupe (1 melon)

1 pound celery (1 bunch, 8 to 12 ribs)

1 pound green beans

1 pound lemons and/or limes (about 7)

Bread/Flour/Rice/Beans/Pasta

$2^1/2$ pounds fresh bread (2 loaves)

1 box Bisquick ($2^1/2$ pounds)

$2^1/2$ pounds bagels (about 20)

2 pounds cornmeal

$1^1/2$ pounds English muffins (12 muffins)

1 pound rolled oats

1 pound wild rice

1 pound dried beans

1 pound lentils

1 pound pasta

Snacks/Desserts

2 pounds mixed nuts

2 pounds chocolate (ten $3^1/2$-ounce bars)

$1^1/4$ pounds peanut butter (one 20-ounce plastic jar)

$1^1/4$ pounds jam or preserves (one 20-ounce plastic jar)

$1^1/4$ pounds pickles (one 20-ounce plastic jar)

1 pound marshmallows

1 pound dried soup mix (about eight 2-ounce packets)

Beverages

$1^1/2$ pounds coffee

$1/2$ pound tea (about 50 tea bags)

$1/2$ pound cocoa

$1/4$ pound powdered fruit drink, such as Kool-Aid (sixteen
   $1/4$-ounce packets; will make 32 quarts)

Condiments

2 pounds (1 quart) cooking oil

$1^1/2$ pounds maple syrup (one 24-ounce plastic bottle)

1 pound sugar

$3/4$ pound ketchup (one 12-ounce plastic bottle)

3/4 pound mayonnaise (one 12-ounce plastic jar)
1/2 pound mustard (one 8-ounce plastic jar)

SERVINGS PER POUND

Suggested servings on food labels aren't much help to a camp cook. As a practical matter, food manufacturers are pretty much free to suggest any serving size they like as long as they also specify its approximate weight and calorie content. This makes provisioning by label for a camping trip an extraordinarily frustrating Alice-Through-the-Looking-Glass exercise.

A labeled "serving" of store-bought sliced bread, for example, generally consists of a single 1-ounce slice containing 70 calories. A labeled "serving" of pasta, on the other hand, weighs 2 ounces and contains 210 calories. A "serving" of canned fruit weighs 4 ounces yet contains only 90 calories. A "serving" of canned tuna fish weighs 2.4 ounces but contains no more calories than a 1-ounce slice of bread. And so it goes—on and on.

Following the labels would convince you that a loaf of bread makes 20 servings, a pound of pasta 8, a can of fruit 4, and a diminutive 6-ounce tin of tuna 2 1/2. In civilization, that's a stretch. Hungry in the outback, it's laughable.

Don't drive yourself crazy trying to decipher the "serving-speak" on food packaging. Forget what the labels "suggest." Based on experience, here's pretty much what a pound of various kinds of provisions will make in camp—and how far they'll go to satisfy camp-sized appetites.

POUNDWISE GUIDE (YIELDS FOR ONE POUND)

1 pound ground coffee - 50 cups (more than 3 gallons) of strong coffee. On most camping trips (two adults for

three to four days), at 3 cups per person per day, 6 to 8 ounces of ground coffee is plenty.

1 pound tea (loose) = 112 cups (about 7 gallons). That's an ocean of tea: more than enough to last four addicted tea drinkers for a week. Individual foil-wrapped tea bags (.09 ounce per bag)—normally sold 12, 20, or 32 teabags to a box—are a better way to go.

1 pound freeze-dried coffee = 224 cups

1 pound sugar = 64 teaspoons

1 pound Bisquick = 21 pancakes or 12 biscuits or 15 dumplings

1 pound sliced bacon = approximately 14 slices

1 loaf sliced bread ($1^{1}/4$ pounds) = approximately 20 slices or enough for 10 sandwiches

1 pound dried beans = 8 camper-sized helpings

1 pound pasta = 4 camper-sized helpings

1 pound rice = 4 camper-sized helpings

1 pound potatoes = 3 medium potatoes or 3 camper-sized helpings

1 pound rolled oats = 14 helpings

1 pound dried fruit = 12 camper-sized helpings

1 pound canned stew or ravioli/spaghetti = 2 small helpings

1 pound dried soup mix = 16 cups or about 8 camper-sized helpings

1 pound (15.75 ounces) canned fruit or vegetable = 2 small helpings

1 can (10.75 ounces) condensed soup = 2 small helpings ($1^{1}/4$ cups)

1 can Spam (12 ounces) = 3 camper-sized helpings

1 can tuna (6 ounces) = 2 small helpings

CHAPTER 5

THE COOK KIT

Essentials

*Our cooking furniture was a tea kettle, one large kettle
to cook in, a frying pan, and some tinned plates.*

—EXPLORER ALEXANDER MACKENZIE, 1790

THOUGH HARD to imagine today, the outfit Mackenzie described was carefully calculated to cook for ten men. The kettles, made of copper (the ultralight metal of the day), nested together for easy transport. The two-gallon tea kettle, with close-fitting lid, quickly brought 32 cups of strong brew to a boil. The cook kettle—more accurately a cauldron—held eight to ten gallons. The cast-iron frying pan was big, too: 15 inches in diameter, with a handle fully four feet long, so it could be safely maneuvered in the hottest fire.

Camp cooking is considerably simpler today than it was back then. Camp cookware, however, has grown increasingly more complicated.

Modern Camp Cook Kit

Nowadays, you can choose from a truly bewildering plethora of camp cook kits, fashioned in virtually every material and configuration you can name. Generally speaking, however, most are made of aluminum—either anodized (hardened) or nonstick coated (with Teflon, DuraLite, BlackLite)—or stainless steel or titanium. As a general rule, aluminum cook kits are lighter than steel, but not as strong. Steel cook kits are heavier than aluminum, but are far more durable. Titanium cook kits are far more expensive than aluminum or steel, yet weigh one-third to one-half as much as either, and rank between the two in durability.

Weightwise, the difference between the lightest (titanium) and heaviest (steel) general-purpose cook kits is somewhat less than a pound (13 ounces, in fact). Costwise, however, the titanium kit costs a phenomenal 265 percent more than its stainless steel twin. The weight difference between the titanium and aluminum kits is even less—barely five ounces, or the equivalent of a medium potato. Still, the titanium kit costs 160 to 257 percent more.

What you're paying for with titanium, of course, is the expensive metallurgy and engineering involved in minimizing weight while preserving performance. That is all well and good in the design of jet aircraft and spaceships (titanium's original purpose). Its cost benefit in camp cook kits—beyond ultralight bragging rights—is another matter.

Culinarily, the differences among aluminum, stainless steel, and titanium cookware—in my experience, anyway—are simple. Aluminum heats fast and tends to burn foods just as quickly unless the cook pays close attention. Steel disperses heat more slowly and evenly, and is more forgiving. Titanium heats slower than either and holds a steady cooking temperature longer, but foods tend to stick to it, even when it has a nonstick coating, so it's usually the hardest to clean.

BEST ALL-PURPOSE CAMP COOK KIT

For the average camper on a budget, aluminum or steel cook kits work just fine, for a fraction of the expense of titanium models. If you go camping a lot, stainless steel is probably a better choice. It will take a lot more abuse, stand up to the fiendish heat of gas stoves and wood fires better, and generally outlive anodized or coated aluminum.

To accommodate a party of two to four persons, a nesting cook kit (bowls, pots, and pans sized to fit one inside the other) containing the following items will serve admirably.

1 frying pan/pot lid (at least 8 inches in diameter and
  2 inches deep)
One $2^1/_2$-quart pot
One $1^1/_2$-quart pot
One 1-quart pot
1 pot gripper
1 spatula (optional)

Each camper should carry his or her own cup, bowl, and spoon. Cups should be metal for one obvious reason: they don't melt like plastic. You can set a metal cup on the stove and cook in it, if you have to. Bowls are better than plates because they function as both. Knives and forks are superfluous. Every camper necessarily carries a jackknife. A spoon or "spork" (a spoon with short tines) is all that's required in the cutlery line.

The one item in any lightweight, nesting cook kit that invariably falls short is the frying pan. Read on.

THE IRREPLACEABLE IRON SKILLET

The bush plane had just disappeared over the treeline, not to return for a week, when I discovered the outpost camp bare of useful cookware. There was only detritus: remnants of Boy Scout mess kits, flaking Teflon fry pans, pitted aluminum pots. Good for burning food, not cooking it. But—hanging on the wall in all its glory—was a big, blackened, oiled iron skillet. It was the only utensil in camp that had been accorded such a high place—and with very good reason.

It's made for campfire cooking. A cast-iron skillet is heavy (a 10-inch pan weighs five pounds) and thick-walled (3/16th inch); built to tame the extreme temperatures of open flames and red-hot coals. It heats evenly (no hot spots or scorching) and holds a steady cooking temperature for a long time— things steel and aluminum cookware don't do. Forged to take the heat, it won't warp like stainless steel or burn through like thin aluminum. Indeed, making the most of open fires is an iron skillet's pedigree and purpose.

It will cook anything. For frying, braising, or sautéing, there's no finer (or more forgiving) pan for a campfire cook. A middle-of-the-road-sized skillet (10 inches wide, 2 inches deep) will easily boil a quart of soup, sauce, or stew. A skillet 3 inches deep will deep-fry, poach, or steam pretty much whatever you like. With a pie tin and aluminum foil, it also makes a very serviceable bake oven: evenly sprinkle some pebbles in the skillet, set the pie tin (filled with cornbread, biscuits, scalloped potatoes, cookies) on top, cover tightly with foil, and place the skillet on hot coals. There's no more versatile instrument for cooking over fire.

It improves with age. The more an iron skillet's "seasoned" and used, the better it gets. Proper seasoning turns it black and forms a durable, protective carbon coating that prevents sticking and burning, stops rust, and imparts a wonderful flavor. The initial three-step seasoning process is easy. (1) With a paper towel, lightly wipe the skillet with a thin coat of vegetable oil, not butter or margarine (see "Dos and Don'ts About Iron Skillets" on page 76). (2) Put it in a 350°F oven for one hour. (3) Remove carefully (it'll be smoking hot), let cool, dry, and wipe it again with a coating of oil. After each use, just clean (see "Dos and Don'ts") and give it another thin wiping of vegetable oil.

Why season an iron skillet? When molten iron is poured into a mold (cast) and cools, air bubbles leave microscopic pores in its surface. Unseasoned, those pores are an iron skillet's Achilles' heel: gateway to corrosion, rust, and hot spots. An application of vegetable oil fills the pores. At high heat, it carbonizes (blackens) to form a very tough nonstick, rust-free, practically wash-free protective coating.

It's economical and will outlive you. Cast-iron cookware's a bargain. A new $10^{1}/2$-inch skillet costs only about $10. Properly cared for, it will outlive you and your great-grandchildren.

It's been on the top 10 camp list forever. On his "long hunts," Daniel Boone took an iron "spider"—a three-legged, long-handled skillet. On his Maine canoe treks (cooking for three), Thoreau took only two pieces of cookware: a four-quart tin kettle for brewing tea and an iron frying pan for everything else. Emigrants following the California and Oregon trails were advised that every party carry at least "one frying pan of wrought iron."

Part of the reason was durability: cast iron's hard, nonmalleable, and, but for rust, all but indestructible—ideal for life in the bush. Mostly though, it was sheer culinary practicality:

no one piece of cookware did so much so well, with minimal maintenance. That's still true today.

DOS AND DON'TS ABOUT IRON SKILLETS

Don't season with salted fat. That means no margarine, salted butter, salt pork, or bacon fat. Salt in the pores of an unseasoned cast-iron skillet causes corrosion, eating pits in the metal.

Avoid cooking acidic foods at first. Until seasoned (five or six uses), don't use your skillet to cook tomatoes or other high-acid foods. Acid in the pores of cast iron will cause corrosion too.

Don't go near the water. Put away those steel scouring pads and abrasive cleaning powders: they'll just denude your carefully seasoned skillet of its protective coating. Don't soak in soapy water (or any water, for that matter): it will jump-start massive rust. You don't really need to wash a seasoned cast-iron skillet at all (which is another reason these things were beloved on the frontier). Just pour some boiling water in it, scrub with a stiff-bristled brush, wipe dry, apply a thin coating of oil, and leave it alone. Counterintuitively, this isn't unsanitary. The boiling-water scrub will fairly sterilize it and reheating it over hot coals before use will kill any remaining bacteria as effectively as a hospital operating room sterilizer.

Get the right size for your party. Diameter and depth are the key measures to consider when buying an iron skillet for camp cooking. Skillets come in a dizzying variety of diameters: from $6^{1}/2$ to $15^{1}/2$ inches (with models of 8, $8^{3}/4$, 9, $9^{1}/2$, 10, $10^{1}/2$, 12, and 15 inches in between). Depths range too: $1^{3}/4$, 2, $2^{1}/2$, 3, $3^{1}/4$ inches, and up.

The Chuck Wagon

★

Legendary Texas trail boss Charles Goodnight (1836–1929) reputedly devised this remarkable advance in field cooking. To drive his cattle from the Llano Estacado (Staked Plains) of central Texas to railheads in Wyoming (Cheyenne) and, later, Colorado (Denver), where they fetched a premium price, he and his partner pioneered the Loving-Goodnight Trail: an 800-mile track across some of the most rugged, waterless country in the West. To feed 20 to 30 cowboys on the three-month journey, he improvised an ingenious, self-contained, traveling kitchen/commissary: one of the first, and arguably best, of its kind.

Goodnight designed it around a surplus U.S. Army wagon that he'd bought on the cheap. These wagons, made to rigid military specifications, had a carrying capacity of 2,000 pounds, were built of the best-seasoned wood, reinforced with iron straps at all stress points, and had nearly unbreakable iron axles. Though they could carry a ton, they were made light and small enough to be drawn by either a two- or four-mule team, instead of the usual six-mule team. By U.S. Army Quartermaster General's directions, the wagon box was but 3 feet 4 inches wide, 1 foot 9 inches deep, and 9 feet 6 inches long at the bottom and 10 feet long at the top. For maximum clearance over rough ground, however, the wheels were made comparatively huge: the front wheels were 3 feet 8 inches in diameter and the rear wheels 4 feet 8 inches high. Wheel rims were armored in iron plate, 2 inches wide and $1/2$ inch thick. All wheels turned on cast-iron hubs and factory forged, hand-hammered iron axles. To shelter the wagon's contents and driver from rain and sun, it was fitted with five bows and a canvas top. Beneath the driver's seat was a built-in toolbox. Under the tailgate, suspended from chains, was a feed box for the wagon's team. Beside the driver's seat was a ratchet-controlled brake.

Fully loaded, such a well-designed, ruggedly built wagon could travel 20 miles a day, more than enough to outpace the 10 to 12 miles per day of the herd and make camp ahead of it every night. What's more, the wagon could do it over the worst terrain. With nearly 2 feet of clearance, it could roll over most obstacles in its path. It could ford water 3 feet deep without wetting its wagon box. Drawn by a good team, it could negotiate grades too steep for a modern farm tractor.

None of that, however, was good enough for Goodnight. Long parts of his trail (a dreaded 90-mile section especially) were bone-dry. So to each side of the wagon, secured by iron straps, he attached water barrels to provide cooking and drinking water when no water was to be found. In the back, he spiked a "grub box"—a compartmentalized unit 3 feet wide by 4 feet high that was part shelves, part slide-out drawers—to furnish immediate access to every necessity required to feed cowhands and watch over or defend the herd. It featured a hinged face that folded down, supported by chains and cleverly folding legs, which made a fine 3 by 4-foot table upon which to prepare meals. In one corner of this fold-down table, Goodnight bolted a coffee grinder, so the all-important device was ever-ready and never lost. On the sides of the grub box, Goodnight bolted a prodigious number of heavy hooks to hang or dry everything from iron skillets, slab bacon, and jerked beef to wet socks, shirts, and long underwear. Hinged atop the grub box, swing-out iron rods provided ready hanging places for lanterns, buckets, canteens, and utensils.

Oddly, the grub box itself usually contained little food. It was packed instead with cookware (Dutch ovens, kettles, skillets, mixing basins), precious condiments (vinegar, molasses, sugar, salt, pepper), a crock of sourdough starter (essential for bread and biscuit making), lanterns (for keeping night watch), waterproof mason jars containing matches, and Colt revolvers, ammunition, whiskey, and tobacco.

Provisions—flour, salt pork, bacon, dried beans, green coffee, dried apples, baking powder—rode in the wagon bed. Trail cook Oliver Nelson, who drove a similar chuck wagon on a cattle drive in 1880, was amazed at what it could carry. By his precise accounting, it contained 1,000 pounds flour, 500 pounds salt pork, 200 pounds dried beans, 160 pounds green coffee beans, 100 pounds sugar, 50 pounds dried apples, 50 pounds salt, 40 pounds lard, 35 pounds baking soda, and some potatoes, dried corn, and raisins. This somewhat exceeded the wagon's carrying capacity, but there was no helping it. Nelson—the sole cook—had 30 ravenous men to feed and a two-month, 600-mile drive ahead. To accommodate the food, he had to make do with a bare minimum of cooking gear. His inventory listed just two Dutch ovens ("16 inches wide and 5 inches deep"), one long-handled iron skillet, one coffeepot, and two tin mixing basins. His only utensils were two knives, one carving fork, and one long-handled spoon.

In the grub box, he discovered a stark assortment of nonedible essentials—among them 12 Colt .45 caliber revolvers and 20 boxes of .45 caliber cartridges. The ammunition amounted to over 40 rounds per revolver, more than the U.S. cavalry at the time issued troopers going into combat. To keep night watch over the herd, there were six bull's-eye lanterns and ten gallons of tinned kerosene. For lantern lighting and fire making, however, there was only one "caddy" of friction matches. In a padlocked compartment, to which only the trail boss had a key, was a two-gallon stoneware jug of "skull pop," or whiskey. Finally, the box held 40 pounds of Climax Plug tobacco (which could be chewed or smoked in a pipe) and 20 pounds of Bull Durham tobacco (the fine-cut cigarette tobacco cowboys used to roll their own).

Amazingly, the little ten-foot wagon—America's first field kitchen—neatly accommodated all of it.

For a party of four, a $10\frac{1}{2}$-inch skillet, 2 inches deep, will do nicely. For larger parties (up to seven), a 12-inch skillet, $2\frac{1}{2}$ inches deep, should be sufficient for most purposes. For parties of eight or more, a jumbo 15-inch skillet, $3\frac{1}{4}$ inches deep (or two 12-inch skillets) is warranted.

Get a handle on it. Sitting close to coals hot enough to melt lead, any size iron skillet gets fiendishly hot. That's why skillets in the 1700s and 1800s typically had a long (2- to 3-foot) handle. That's not the case today. My $10\frac{1}{2}$-inch skillet has a handle only $4\frac{3}{4}$ inches long. Longer-hinged (folding), wood-covered handles are available on some models, but they're still perilously short (and a world less secure than cast-metal handles). The best remedy is to purchase a "hot handle holder": an insulated sleeve, similar to an oven mitt, that fits over the skillet handle. At about $2.50 apiece, you'll be glad you did.

Don't toss it because of rust. Iron, as well as steel, skillets will rust if not cared for or subjected to the usual punishment of field use (left out in the rain, upset in a canoe capsize, etc.). Flea markets and garage sales are littered with rusty but otherwise perfectly sound (and dirt-cheap) iron skillets. Usually, this coating is no more than a cosmetic surface rime of rust and is easily removed. Simply scour with a steel or copper pad and scouring powder, wash with soap and water, towel dry, and place in a hot oven for 30 minutes. Reseason it before using and it's ready to go.

IT WILL DO MORE THAN COOK

An iron skillet's one of the original multipurpose tools. It makes an excellent fish bonker, nut cracker, garlic press, or sledgehammer (for driving tent stakes or splitting wood). Fill a skillet with hot coals for ten minutes, empty, and it makes a very good iron. Bang it with a heavy spoon, it's a signal bell. One pioneer, attempting to make a fire in a downpour, recollected that by "putting on the frying pan bottom up, I had an iron umbrella and a bright fire in spite of the rain."

You have to love cookware like that.

PART III

Breakfasts, Breads, and Brews

★ CHAPTER 6 ★

BREAKFASTS

Old-Timers' Ways to Start the Day

Nothing improves scenery like ham and eggs.

—MARK TWAIN, 1874

IN ANY camp, morning is invariably the coldest time of day. Temperatures, which generally drop throughout the night, usually bottom out about sunrise. That makes a hot, hearty breakfast especially welcome. Today's cold cereals, juice drinks, and energy bars can't compare to old-fashioned hot breads, fried ham or fish, and steaming coffee.

⟩⟩⟩⟩⟩ Johnnycake ⟨⟨⟨⟨⟨

Serves 4

On the American frontier, this flat frypan bread was originally called "journey cake," because it was the staple of long hunters on extended forays into the wild. The original recipe involved no more than stone-ground cornmeal, bacon drippings, and boiling water. Minimally updated, it's still about the best, quickest, and heartiest breakfast you can make in the outdoors. Indeed, if you're frying bacon and making coffee, it's effortless.

1 cup stone-ground white cornmeal
1 teaspoon salt
1 tablespoon butter
1 tablespoon sugar
$\frac{1}{4}$ cup milk
Bacon drippings
Butter for serving
Maple syrup, honey, molasses, or sorghum for serving

In a mess tin, combine the cornmeal, salt, butter, and sugar. Add about a cup of boiling water (from the pot you're boiling to make coffee), then the milk, and mix well into a thick batter.

Heat bacon drippings in a skillet. Drop the batter by tablespoons, like pancakes, into the skillet. With fork or spatula, flatten the batter to about $\frac{1}{2}$ inch thick. Cook over coals (medium heat, if you're using a range) until golden brown on one side (5 to 6 minutes). Flip and brown the other side. Serve with plenty of butter, maple syrup, or honey—or molasses or sorghum, if you want to go old school.

>>>>> Fried Ham and Red-eye Gravy <<<<<

For those north of the Mason-Dixon Line, this legendary Southern camp recipe bears mention. The reddish glaze and drippings from the ham give the gravy its name. Some mix coffee with the drippings to make "black-eye" gravy (a morning eye-opener and uncommonly good). It made a rib-sticking breakfast for long hunters like Daniel Boone and Davy Crockett. The cured ham keeps without refrigeration and travels well. In the woods, there's nothing simpler to make and—however shaky your cooking skills—it cannot be made badly. Children seem to enjoy helping turn the ham and stir the gravy.

1 to 2 slices country-cured ham ($^{1}/_{3}$ pound) per person

Cut a couple of thin ($^{1}/_{4}$ inch or less) slices off a country ham. Carefully. Slicing anything thin in the bush results in more needless, self-inflicted injuries than any other cause I know of. Always cut *away from* and not *toward* your fingers.

Trim some fat from the edges and render (melt) it in a skillet over medium heat. Add the sliced ham and cook about 5 minutes a side, turning frequently.

Remove the ham from the skillet, pour in $^{1}/_{2}$ cup water (or coffee for black-eye gravy), and simmer about 3 minutes, scraping the meat and fat dredgings from the bottom of the skillet and stirring.

Drizzle gravy over the ham and sop it up with frypan bread or biscuits.

››››› Hot-Water Corn Pone ‹‹‹‹‹

Serves 4

Cornmeal and camp have gone together forever. Kept cool and dry, cornmeal will keep quite well, unrefrigerated, for months. Mixed with plain water, it makes a dense, wonderfully flavorful frypan bread. In Algonquian, it was called *apan* (AH-pone) which, roughly translated, means baked; the Indians baked the corn dough in the hot ashes of their fires. Generations of explorers, hunters, pioneers, and homesteaders, who more or less lived on the dish, called it pone.

On camping trips "back of beyond" today, fresh-made pone is as good and easy to make as it ever was. Try it.

2 cups self-rising yellow cornmeal
3 tablespoons all-purpose flour
1 teaspoon salt
2 tablespoons sugar
Butter, jam, or honey for serving

Heat a greased skillet.

In a mess tin, mix the dry ingredients. Add just enough hot water to make a thick, gummy batter. Form into patties by hand. Fry in the hot skillet, turning once, until golden brown. Just plain good.

››››› Campfire Cornbread ‹‹‹‹‹

Serves 4

While corn pone was a staple backwoods dish, real cornbread signified a richer, more civilized camp. Though it's little more than pone made with milk and eggs, that little difference means a lot. Well-made cornbread, crowning a black iron skillet in camp, is gourmet fare. It can be cooked in a reflector oven in front of a campfire, in a camp oven on a range, or in a conventional oven at 450°F. Serve with butter or margarine or jam or honey.

3 cups self-rising cornmeal
1 teaspoon salt

2 tablespoons bacon grease or oil, plus extra for greasing
the skillet
1^1/2 cups milk
2 large eggs

Preheat the oven to 450°F. Grease an iron skillet or tin.

In a bowl, mix the cornmeal and salt. In a separate bowl, blend the grease, milk, and eggs. Mix the wet and dry ingredients, pour into the pan, and bake for 20 minutes. Serve hot.

>>>>> Fish Cakes <<<<<

Serves 2

The best thing to do with any leftover cooked fish (whether fried, broiled, baked, or boiled) is make it into fish cakes. At night, they're a savory side dish. The morning after a fish dinner, they're fantastic for breakfast.

1 cup leftover fish
1 large egg
^{1}/2 cup leftover mashed potatoes
^{1}/2 cup diced onion
1 to 2 tablespoons all-purpose flour
Vegetable oil for frying (about ^{1}/4 cup)

In a bowl, mash the leftover fish with a fork. Add the egg, potatoes, onion, and flour and stir well. Heat the oil in a skillet, form the fish mixture into patties, and fry like pancakes, until golden brown on each side.

COWBOY COOKS AND COOKING

★

In 1880, a 19-year-old ranch hand named Oliver Nelson took the only job he could find on the Oklahoma Range—trail cook on cattle drive. The fact that he knew nothing about cooking—and said so—didn't seem to matter to the outfit that hired him. They needed a man, he needed work, they shook hands on it, and that was that.

"I rode down the Chisholm Trail south," he wrote later, "and turned off when I reached the camp. A bald-headed fellow with dirty overalls and low shoes—kind of a hard looker—was washing a black kettle with a rag almost as black. I told him, 'I've hired to the Carter outfit to cook.'

"He threw the kettle one way, the rag the other, wiped his hands on his breeches, put on his hat, took the reins out of my hands and swung into the saddle. I asked, 'What am I supposed to do?' He said, 'You're the cook,' and rode off toward town in a lope."

Nelson, of necessity, was forced to learn the craft (art, actually) of camp cooking the hard way. He taught himself to be an excellent one. Perhaps it was because he was so young. Most trail cooks at the time tended to be men well into middle age or beyond. Usually they were former cowboys, hobbled by injuries (too many mule kicks, bucking mustangs, and angry bulls) or suffering rheumatism and arthritis from a life spent working on the open range. In the vernacular of the day, they were "used up." Many, in self-medicating their aches and pains and dark future, were what today are called functional alcoholics. Trail cook was the end of the line for a cowboy; indeed, only the solitary labor of "riding fence" was worse. Cooking for 20 to 30 men, twice a day, for months on end, was enough to break a sound man. It was the last job a washed-up cowboy wanted and the last job he was likely to have.

Trail cooks didn't have many provisions to work with: usually only flour, bacon, dried beans, sugar, salt, lard, baking soda, and green coffee beans, and perhaps potatoes and dried fruit. It doesn't seem possible that such mundane stuff could be made palatable, much less interesting. But an experienced trail cook knew how to make monotonous fare varied and short rations last.

A good cook, according to one cowboy, could turn out flour biscuits "five inches high, real light and crusted over with sugar," "spatter dabs" (flapjacks), "huck dummy" (frypan bread with raisins), "boggy top pie" (dried apples stewed with sugar and baked into a pie with only a bottom crust), and "son-of-a-bitch sack" (dried fruit rolled in dough, wrapped in cheesecloth, and boiled or steamed like dumplings). A good cook fried flour-coated salt pork into what was called "Kansas City fish," stewed it with dried corn into what was called "hog trough," or baked it with beans and molasses into "Boston pot." He boiled beans to make what cowboys called "music soup," mashed and fried them to make frijoles, or simmered them with beef to make chili. If he was without butter, he substituted "Charlie Taylor" (a mixture of molasses and bacon grease). He turned potatoes into "prairie pickles" (sliced potatoes soaked overnight in salt water, drizzled with vinegar, and served raw).

Ironically, on cattle drives cooks had little beef to supplement the menu. "Blue meat" (young, tender calves, born along the way and unable to keep up) and "slow elk" (strays from other herds) went into the pot. But full-grown, fattened steers were killed only as a necessity. Every one killed cost the outfit money and—lacking time or means to preserve 500 pounds of raw meat—most of it was wasted. Choice pieces were cut into steaks and immediately fried in bacon grease until they were well done (no cowboy cottoned to bloody meat). The remainder was "jerked"—sliced thin, Indian style, and hung in the sun to dry. A supply of this furnished a trail cook with materials for "jowler"—a stew of dried beef, slow-boiled to plumpness, thickened with flour, and sparked with plenty of salt and pepper—that was a great favorite on the range.

How to Brew Great Camp Coffee

There is perhaps no outdoor topic more subjective or contro-versial—or homicidally charged at 5 a.m.—than how best to make camp coffee. Specifically, I'm talking about coffee brewed over a wood fire or camp stove in a plain, blackened pot, without benefit of percolators, drip baskets, presses, or other devices. Just coffee, made the old-fashioned, time-honored camp way.

The maddening thing is that it seems so simple. It takes only two ingredients, after all: coffee and boiling water. But it's more complicated than that. To ensure perfect camp brew, follow these rules.

RULE 1: STICK TO WHOLE-BEAN COFFEE

Leave that ground coffee on the supermarket shelves alone (whether it's bagged, canned, or vacuum-packed). Not only is it usually a cheaper blend of young and old beans that tend toward bitterness, it's preground. That convenience comes at a price. Once the seal is broken, it will lose up to 50 percent of its flavorful coffee oils within as little as 18 to 24 hours. After a few days in the bush, it'll make a cup of hot, brown water, but not much else.

Buy whole-bean roast coffee. It smells heavenly and natu-rally preserves flavor and taste. Take it from the bag you bought it in and pack it in an airtight container, like a Nalgene bottle. Don't refrigerate or stash it in a camp cooler: the resulting condensation can ruin your choice, dry-roasted beans.

RULE 2: GET THE RIGHT ROAST

It's the roasting that develops and preserves the more than 800 substances in a coffee bean—especially its essential fla-vor and aroma-producing oils. Roasts range from light to medium brown (medium is the standard for most American coffee drinkers), to very dark Italian roasts and burnt, almost black French roasts. Almost more than the bean, the roast will determine that tartness, aroma, and body of any coffee you choose.

If your camp mates are like most of us, pick a medium roast. If they're espresso fanciers, pick a darker roast. As a rule of thumb, the darker the roast, the stronger, fuller, and more robust the flavor.

RULE 3: GRIND IT FINE

Minutes before brewing, grind the beans fine. The finer the grind, the more particles (surface area) and coffee oils are exposed to the water, releasing more aroma and flavor. On the other hand, too fine a grind can make the brew bitter.

If you don't have a grinder in camp, wrap the beans in a bandanna and pulverize them with the butt of an axe or a fish bonker. This will produce a coarser grind that'll take a bit more time to surrender its flavor, but more about that later.

RULE 4: USE GOOD WATER

Your carefully selected, roasted, stored, and ground beans can be ruined in the flick of a whitetail's flag by a pot of bad water. Well water can be full of untasty minerals. A canteen of tap water from home is chlorinated.

Use fresh spring, brook, or lake water, if you can get it (and are sure of the source). If not, bottled water is fine and no harder to tote than a canteen of tap water. These will dramatically improve the taste of the brew. So will carefully cleaning the pot after each brewing.

RULE 5: KNOW YOUR STRENGTH

How strong or mild camp mates like their coffee is highly individual. What's more, it probably varies during the day. In the morning, they may want an eye-opener. In the evening, they may want a gentler brew.

Opinion here—like everything else in this murky process—varies widely. Some say 2 teaspoons of ground coffee per each cup of water will do nicely. Others say 1 heaping tablespoon (equivalent to 3 teaspoons) per cup of water, plus 1 extra tablespoon "for the pot" is required. Still others maintain you should fill the pot with water, toss in two handfuls of ground coffee, and that's that.

Generally speaking, I favor the handful approach (it's a hell of lot easier first thing in the morning). Experiment here until you find the right strength to satisfy all hands. Your camp mates will provide plenty of feedback, no doubt.

RULE 6: BREW WISELY

There are two time-tested—eternally debatable—ways to go. Choose wisely. Once committed, there's no going back.

Woodsman's Coffee: Take a good medium-roast, middle-of-the-road, whole-bean coffee (like Mocha Java, which you'll commonly find in your local supermarket) and grind it coarse. Adherents to this method insist it must be coarse-ground or it will be ruined in the brewing. Drop 2 tablespoons of coffee into the pot and pour in 6 cups of cold water.

Set the pot over coals and slowly bring to a gentle, not rolling, boil. Immediately remove from heat and let steep for about 5 minutes. Before pouring, add 3 to 4 tablespoons of cold water to settle the grounds (which works surprisingly well).

This makes some very strong—chewy, in fact—coffee. Taken black, it may be too hair-raising for all but die-hard coffee drinkers. Indeed, it's well deserving of its various camp nicknames: mule kick, Missouri mud, and mustang. I find it overwhelmingly strong, muddy, and bitter. Others don't. Many up-at-4-a.m. hunters and anglers say the stuff's just what's needed at that ungodly hour. To tame it a bit for milder tastes, add a packet of instant cocoa to the pot before serving.

Cowboy Coffee: Adherents of this method insist that the preceding technique—boiling the coffee and water together—ruin it. I agree wholeheartedly. The hard boil, if it doesn't drive the grounds out of the pot like hot lava, vaporizes the beans' fragrant, flavorful oils, sending the brew's flavor up in smoke.

Adding the grind to boiling water after it's removed from the fire preserves its aroma and taste. It's simply done.

Fill a coffeepot or kettle with 6 cups of cold water and bring to a screeching boil, the hotter the better. Remove from heat, throw in 2 handfuls of ground coffee (about $1/2$ cup, if you want to get fussy about it), stir with a stick, and cover. Let steep for 3 minutes, add 3 to 4 tablespoons of cold water to settle the grounds, and pour at once.

This produces a much tastier, milder, and clearer brew. It's still brawny coffee, but cowboys drank it by the gallon.

If all else fails—when the wood is wet, the propane is gone, or the last bean has vanished—there's still one alternative. Called Night Nurse's Nirvana, it requires only a cup. The recipe's the simplest of all: yesterday's coffee, drunk cold and black.

It's better than no coffee at all.

CAMP COFFEE TIPS

1. One pound of fresh-ground coffee will make about 50 cups (or 3.1 cups per ounce). How much to take on a camping trip? According to the U.S. Department of Agriculture, the typical American drinks 1.64 cups of coffee daily. For campers, figure 3 cups (or 1 ounce ground coffee) per person per day.

2. Leave the instant coffee behind. Nobody really likes it.

3. Be sure to pack sugar/sweeteners and milk/cream (real or artificial)—63 percent of coffee drinkers want theirs with one or the other or both. Only 37 percent of coffee drinkers like it black.

4. An efficient thermos bottle can keep coffee hot (or at least warm) for as long as three days. And an insulated mug will keep your brew hot far longer than metal or enameled cups. See the Camp Cook's Directory (page 250) for various suppliers.

Finally, if old fashioned camp-made coffee's too plain for you, there are all kinds of new-fangled, lightweight coffee-making devices out there (from French presses to espresso makers). See the Camp Cook's Directory (page 247) for manufacturers.

★ Chapter 7 ★

THE REAL STUFF

Traditional Camp Breads

We have been out of bread a few days
and begin to miss it more than seems reasonable,
for we have plenty of meat and sugar and tea.
Strange we could feel so food-poor
in so rich a wilderness.

—JOHN MUIR, 1869

ACK OF bread has probably sparked more mutinies, riots, and revolutions—and destroyed more dynasties and empires (and camping trips)—than anything else on mankind's menu. Perhaps that's because bread, more than any other human food, is the embodiment of satiety, safety, and security—in other words, home.

Take away bread in camp for even a "few days," however, and most of us (like Muir) turn into cry babies in the woods.

Best Store-Bought Breads for Camp

On typical camping trips lasting two to four days, almost any kind of store-bought (or more properly, factory-made) bread you prefer will do. All brands contain various additives to keep them soft, retard staleness and spoilage, and, in their original plastic bags, will remain edible (read: saleable) for up to a week.

The problem with taking soft loaf breads camping is that they seldom survive a trip to camp without being mashed or flattened. Tortillas, on the other hand (another quintessential American camp food), can be carried with no such worries. Indeed, compared to a standard loaf of white or wheat bread (weighing 20 ounces, and containing 20 to 22 slices), a crushproof pack of ten flour tortillas (weighing 15 ounces) occupies roughly one-tenth the space, contains just as many calories (about 1,500), and will keep a week or more.

Dark, dense breads, like fresh rye or pumpernickel, travel well in the bush, keep seven to ten days, and are far more flavorful (a boon in the wild). However, many campers (children especially), weaned on white, cakelike breads, don't like them.

If that's the case, bagels are a happier, healthier, longer-keeping alternative. Bagels—bread made of dough that's been boiled, then baked—typically contain no preservatives whatever. Dense and compact, they're more or less impervious to rough travel in a rucksack or Duluth pack. They'll keep for 10 to 14 days. Plus they're available in a wonderful variety, so you can easily pack a mix that will please far more palates in camp than any one, two, or three kinds of loaf breads you might carry.

Though more like crackers than bread, old standbys like melba toast, zwieback, breadsticks, crispbreads, and hardtack (or its contemporary equivalent, MRE crackers) will certainly serve in its stead. They're far lighter, take up much less room, and keep far longer than any soft bread.

Should whatever store-bought, soft bread you choose go stale, don't feed it to the squirrels. Mash it into crumbs for stuffing or breading fresh fish, or for making bread pudding. Simpler—and to my mind better—just brown some diced garlic in a skillet with some butter or olive oil, and fry the stale bread slices until they're good and crispy on both sides. Serve as an hors d'oeuvre or with hot soup, chowder, or stew. It will be gladly received.

BEST CAMP-MADE BREADS FOR THE BUSH

For years I persisted in packing various kinds of store-bought bread on camping trips. Sooner or later (usually the former), however, it always went stale, moldy, or otherwise bad.

Traditional camp quick breads, on the other hand, don't. Freshly made from flour or cornmeal (see Chapter 6 for cornbread recipe), fragrant and served piping hot, they're gone before anything bad can happen to them. Most are simple, easy, and so much better than any store-bought bread that there's no comparison. Nowadays, even on an overnight backpacking trip, I prefer old-fashioned frypan or bannock to any premade bread from a grocery store. In layover or fixed camps with any kind of oven (whether Dutch, reflector, or propane—see page 106), I'll take fresh-baked flour biscuits, cornbread, or sourdough over any store-bought baked goods you can name.

BANNOCK

"Store bread is for city folks," wrote canoeist and conservationist Sigurd Olson. "Bannock for the bush."

Indeed, bannock—a pancake of flour, baking powder, and

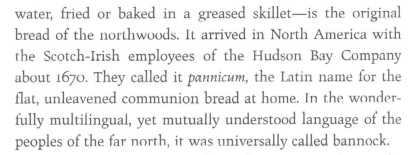

water, fried or baked in a greased skillet—is the original bread of the northwoods. It arrived in North America with the Scotch-Irish employees of the Hudson Bay Company about 1670. They called it *pannicum*, the Latin name for the flat, unleavened communion bread at home. In the wonderfully multilingual, yet mutually understood language of the peoples of the far north, it was universally called bannock.

In his classic book *The Lonely Land*, an account of a month-long canoe trek following the route of the old fur brigades through Saskatchewan, Olson gave as good a description of the method, making, and mystery of this bread as exists anywhere. "That afternoon I made another bannock," he wrote.

> *Taking a cupful of prepared biscuit mix, I added just enough water so I could knead it into a fairly dry ball of dough. The kneading is important, for without it the bread might be too porous. Finally patting the ball into a flat cake, possibly not much more than half an inch in thickness, I pressed it into a well-greased frying pan, browned it gently on each side, then placed it beside the fire where it would catch the heat and bake slowly for half an hour. It is the traditional bread of the North, and Indians and men of the bush vie with each other in method and ingredients, and guard their recipes jealously. Some say that one must start with flour and salt and that prepared mixes are no good, others say that reflector ovens or Dutch ovens are the answer, but most of the men I know stick to the old traditional use of the frying pan.*
>
> *An old-timer once told me that no bannock deserves the name that has neither raisins nor berries in the dough. Another claims that the only way to make the dough is to hollow out a place in the top of a sack of flour, add water, and knead it until it becomes a ball of the proper size and consistency. Flattened out and fried in a pan, it is food for men.*

A crusty, plain bannock, well slathered with butter or jam, is excellent eating. Made with ripe berries (blueberries, blackberries, and raspberries), it's a memorable taste of the wild. Simply add about $^{1}/_{2}$ cup of berries per each cup of flour. Mix them in (gently) after kneading the dough. If you're berry-less, chop some cheese into small chunks and mix into the dough. If you're berry-less and cheesed out, give the dough an authoritative sprinkling of cinnamon or nutmeg.

For such a seemingly simple camp bread, ingredients and methods vary as widely as the individuals making it. Whatever recipe you adopt, you really can't make it badly.

»»»» Bradford Angier's Bannock «««««

Serves 2 to 3

Angier is justifiably famous for his countless books on trekking, camping, and cooking in the bush. His recipe for bannock is worthy of note and among the simplest there is. "Bannock never tastes better than when devoured piping hot around a camp-fire," he wrote, "It should be broken apart, never cut. A cold bannock sliced in half, however, and made into a man-sized sandwich with plenty of meat or other filler in between is the best lunch ever."

1 cup all-purpose flour
1 teaspoon baking powder
$^{1}/_{4}$ tablespoon salt
3 tablespoons margarine

Light a fire and let it burn down to a bed of red-hot coals. In a mess tin, combine the dry ingredients. Cut in the margarine and mix into a coarse meal. Stir in enough cold water (about $^{1}/_{4}$ cup) to make a firm dough. Shape "with as little

In Praise of Good Old Bisquick

★

Whatever camp breads or biscuits you make, good old Bisquick can't be beat. This venerable mix—introduced back in 1930—contains flour, baking soda, salt, and dried buttermilk. This saves campers the time and trouble of packing and mixing the ingredients separately and simplifies making everything from bannock, pancakes, and biscuits to dumplings, cake, and piecrust. It's damned good for coating or battering fish and making skillet gravy, too. The recipes on the box recommend mixing with milk and a fresh egg or two, but plain water does just fine; perfect for camp cooks.

A standard-size box weighs $2^{1}/_{2}$ pounds (approximately 9 cups). In the bush, that will make 4 skillets of bannock, 10 big biscuits, and 14 pancakes, with enough left over to coat and fry a mess of fish. If your tastes run in other directions, the same box will make 10 dumplings for stews or soups, 6 shortcakes, 2 pies, and 1 coffee cake, with enough left to make fruit or vegetable fritters.

handling as possible into a cake about an inch thick," says Angier.

Lay the cake in a greased skillet. Hold over the coals until a bottom crust forms, about 5 minutes. Turn. Remove the skillet from the heat and prop it before the coals, so the top of the cake gets direct heat. Let cook 15 minutes, gradually increasing the angle of the skillet. If the dough flows to one side, you are rushing the process. When a wood splinter inserted in the baked bannock comes out clean, it's done.

Bannock is best served at once, piping hot, exactly as Angier said.

WHOLE WHEAT BANNOCK

Serves 2 to 3

Yet another permutation worth trying.

1 cup whole wheat flour
$^1/_2$ cup all-purpose flour
2 tablespoons baking powder
2 tablespoons sugar
$^1/_2$ teaspoon salt
2 tablespoons butter, margarine, or Crisco

Prepare as for Angier's bannock in the preceding recipe.

OATMEAL BANNOCK

Serves 2 to 3

It goes without saying that this is bread for oatmeal lovers, so query your camp mates beforehand.

3/4 cup rolled oats
3/4 cup whole wheat flour

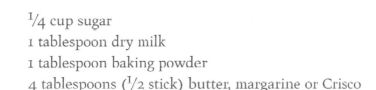

¹/₄ cup sugar
1 tablespoon dry milk
1 tablespoon baking powder
4 tablespoons (¹/₂ stick) butter, margarine or Crisco

Prepare as per Angier's method on pages 102–4.

LEFTOVER BEAN BANNOCK

Serves 4

I know it sounds dreadful, but it's actually quite good: something of a backwoods, one-pan approximation of brown bread and beans. Serve with eggs for breakfast or fried fish for dinner.

1 cup all-purpose flour
1 cup yellow cornmeal
1 tablespoon baking powder
1 teaspoon salt
¹/₂ teaspoon pepper
2 cups cooked leftover beans (with broth), mashed

Combine the dry ingredients in a bowl, add the mashed beans and broth, and mix well into a firm dough. If the bean broth is insufficient and the mixture is too dry, add dribs and drabs of water. Prepare following Angier's method (pages 102–4).

››››› Cornmeal Bannock ‹‹‹‹‹

Serves 2

This is my all-time favorite quick camp bread, especially on backpacking trips. Carried premixed in a zip-lock bag, all you have to do is pour in a little water, knead the bag with your fingers (no messy bowls or hands to wash), cut off a corner of the bag, squeeze the dough into a pan, and cook for five or six minutes.

Technically, this really isn't bannock (which is first browned, then baked by the fire), but frypan bread, which is fried in the pan like a thick pancake, no baking necessary.

Semantics aside, it's the quickest, easiest way to make hot bread in the bush.

2/3 cup yellow cornmeal
1/3 cup all-purpose flour
1 tablespoon baking powder
1 teaspoon salt
Butter, jam, or honey for serving

As with all camp frypan breads, have a nice bed of coals and a greased skillet ready.

In a mess tin, add only enough water to the dry ingredients (1/4 to 1/2 cup) to make a stiff mush. Place the batter in a skillet and pat with a fork or spatula into a thick pancake. Cook over hot coals for 3 to 4 minutes or until golden brown on one side. Turn and cook another 2 minutes.

NOTHING BEATS BISCUITS

Unlike bannock and frypan breads, which require no more than a hot fire and skillet, biscuits are best made in camps with some kind of an oven.

Old-fashioned cast-iron Dutch ovens—universally called "bake ovens" on the frontier—are ideal not only for baking, but also for frying, boiling, stewing, and just about any other culinary endeavor imaginable. They're damnably heavy, however. A 5-quart (12-inch diameter) cast-iron Dutch oven (with lid and lid lifter) weighs almost 12 pounds. A cast aluminum model of the same dimensions weighs 8 pounds. That kind of weight is "luggable" if you're car camping, or canoe-

ℱINE-𝒯UNING ℬANNOCK

★

You can easily tweak the taste and texture of any bannock.

If you prefer a crispier crust, add 1 tablespoon of sugar per each cup of flour or meal. For thickness and richness, add 1 egg (or powdered equivalent) per cup of flour or meal. For more flavor and color, add 1 tablespoon milk per cup (fresh works better). To make bannock softer, add 2 tablespoons of butter or margarine per cup of flour or meal.

---

ing or rafting, and well worth the carriage. If you're backpacking, it's prohibitive.

A number of outdoor equipment suppliers (such as Coleman) make very sturdy, folding camp ovens designed to work on propane stoves or electric hot plates. Typically these weigh 7 to 8 pounds and transform the ubiquitous two-burner portable camp range (weight 11 pounds) into a highly efficient oven. In aggregate, of course, that combination is weightier than an old-fashioned cast-iron Dutch oven. Then again, it's a helluva lot quicker and more convenient to use.

Collapsible reflector ovens have been around forever, and for a lightweight, portable means for baking (or broiling, for that matter), there's little better in the bush. Made of heavy-gauge steel or aluminum, they fold flat and weigh only 4 to 6 pounds. It takes some practice to position them at the proper distance from a fire to bake, instead of burn, their contents, but not much.

Even on ultralight backpacking trips, a biscuit-baking reflector oven is easily improvised. A sheet of heavy-duty aluminum foil, pitched like a miniature lean-to in front of the fire (half forming a floor to hold your dough goods, half rigged as a shed roof at a 45-degree angle above them) will work.

Whichever bake oven suits your circumstance, it serves no better purpose than making a batch of biscuits.

»»»» Easy Camp Biscuits «««

Makes about 10 biscuits

These require no kneading, rolling out, or cutting into shape—just a mixing bowl, greased tin, and hot oven.

  2 cups all-purpose flour
  2 teaspoons baking powder
  2 tablespoons sugar
  1/2 teaspoon salt
  1 large egg, beaten
  1/2 cup milk (or rehydrated dry milk equivalent)
  4 tablespoons (1/2 stick) butter, margarine, or Crisco
    (melted)

Preheat the oven to 425°F. Grease a muffin tin or skillet.

In bowl, mix the flour, baking powder, sugar, and salt. Add the egg, milk, and butter. Stir, but don't overmix. The batter should be lumpy. Spoon into the greased muffin tin. If you don't have a muffin tin in camp, drop spoonfuls onto a skillet (the result will be more of a biscuit loaf than individual biscuits, but will be just as tasty). Bake for about 25 minutes.

›››› Beat-up Biscuits ‹‹‹‹

Makes 15 to 20 biscuits

There are probably a thousand recipes for old-time beaten biscuits. As the name implies, they take a strong arm to make well, but require few ingredients and a modicum of time. They are best made in a layover or fixed camp, or cabin or cottage, where you've got a nice, flat surface to work on.

Serve topped with wafer-thin slices of country ham for an appetizer. Or serve with ham, eggs, and red-eye gravy for breakfast.

4 cups all-purpose flour, plus more for kneading
1/2 teaspoon baking powder
1 teaspoon salt
8 tablespoons (1 stick) butter, margarine, or Crisco, melted
1¼ cups milk

Preheat the oven to 350°F. Generously grease a large baking sheet.

In a bowl, mix all the ingredients and beat the hell out of them with a wooden spoon until the dough is stiff and blistering. Sprinkle in a little more flour, knead lightly on a floured surface, and roll the dough about 1/2 inch thick (a floured beer bottle will serve in lieu of a rolling pin).

Cut into biscuits (use an empty can), poke each with a fork three or four times, and place on the baking sheet. Bake for 20 to 25 minutes or until light golden brown.

>>>>> Sweet Potato Biscuits <<<<<

Makes 15 to 20 biscuits

Mixing a couple of mashed sweet potatoes with the usual biscuit-making material makes something materially different and naturally sweet. For parties surfeited on flour biscuits, these are a welcome, unexpected change-up.

2 cups all-purpose flour, plus more for rolling the dough
1 tablespoon baking powder
1 teaspoon salt
4 tablespoons ($^{1}/_{2}$ stick) butter, margarine, or Crisco
2/3 cup milk
2 cups cooked, mashed sweet potatoes

Preheat the oven to 450°F. Generously grease a large baking sheet.

In a bowl, combine the flour, baking powder, and salt. Cut in the butter with two knives. Add the milk and sweet potatoes and mix into a soft dough.

On a floured surface, roll out $^{1}/_{2}$ inch thick and cut into biscuits, using an empty can as a biscuit cutter. Place on the baking sheet and bake for 15 to 20 minutes.

>>>>> Biscuit Gravy <<<<<

Serves 4

This was—and remains to this day—a staple of original American camp cooking. In frontier, cowboy, and logging camps, it was the hearty, filling mainstay. If it wasn't served up at least once a day, there was generally hell to pay. Fortunately for camp cooks, it was easy—compared to biscuit making. Made with the fat and pan scrapings of any fried meat (bacon, ham, beef, chicken, venison), it required only flour, salt, pepper, and water. Nowadays milk usually takes the place of water.

Pan grease and drippings
2 to 3 tablespoons all-purpose flour
Salt and pepper

In a skillet with pan drippings, mix the flour, salt, and pepper. Stir constantly over medium-high heat until the mixture browns. Add 1 cup water (or milk), stirring, and cook until the gravy bubbles, then simmer, still stirring, until it reaches whatever consistency you like (thin or thick). Serve over biscuits.

OTHER CLASSIC CAMP BREADS

Hudson Bay bread is an invaluable addition to any camper's provisions, while sourdough, the original camp bread, is impractical for all but the most dedicated bakers.

⟩⟩⟩⟩⟩ Hudson Bay Bread ⟨⟨⟨⟨⟨

(from Jim Clark, Canoe Canada Outfitters)

Serves 10 to 12 generously

Jim Clark and Bud Dickson have been outfitting canoeists in Canada's Quetico and White Otter Wilderness areas for over 20 years. Their version of Hudson Bay bread—the legendary dense, long-lasting, power bread of the fur brigades—is a staple in provisioning paddlers. It's quicker and easier to make than most, but just as good. While it can be made in a fixed camp or cabin in less than an hour, it's better made ahead, thrown in the food pack, and eaten for breakfast, lunch, or dinner.

2 cups margarine

2 cups sugar

⅓ cup light corn syrup

⅓ cup honey

9 cups quick-cooking oats

1 cup sweetened flaked coconut

Preheat the oven to 350°F.

Combine all ingredients and press into an oiled jelly-roll pan, until about 3/4 inch thick. Bake for about 25 minutes.

Let the pan cool until you can cut the bread into squares or bars without it breaking. But don't wait too long or it will crumble.

This is the basic recipe. To vary it, add chopped nuts, chocolate chips, molasses, or dried fruit.

Sourdough Bread

★

No book on American camp food and cooking would be complete without mention of sourdough, the staple bread in mining camps from the California gold rush of 1849 to the Klondike gold stampede of the 1890s. Besides fat bacon and black coffee, miners ate little else and so came to be called "sourdoughs" themselves. Like panning or digging for gold, however, making old-fashioned sourdough bread is not easy. Indeed, making it well is something of an art.

The whole reason miners depended on sourdough—bread leavened quite literally with soured dough from a previous baking—was that in their remote camps they had no leavening agents like yeast, baking powder, or baking soda. They had to make their own: a messy, living, breathing culture of bacteria and fungus they called "starter." A mixture of flour, sugar, vinegar, and warm water, left to sour for a week or more, it smelled vile, but raised flapjacks, biscuits, and bread.

Because sourdough starter was less active and slower working (rising) than modern leavening agents, bread baking for the old-timers was usually a daylong, once-a-week affair. It was typically done on Sundays, a day to catch up on chores.

Substituting modern, prepackaged sourdough starter mixes, milk instead of water, and self-rising instead of plain flour speeds things up, but it's still a laborious four- to five-hour process. Unless you're an experienced baker, stick to frypan breads, bannock, and biscuits in camp.

>-<

PART IV

Meat and Fish

CHAPTER 8

MEAT MATTERS

Feeding Carnivores in Camp

If you are cooking from staples as opposed to packaged meals, meat is always the biggest problem.

—CANOEIST/WRITER/ARTIST BILL MASON

FRESH MEAT, unless you're in a camp where it can be stored in a freezer and thawed in a refrigerator, won't keep long. If hard frozen beforehand and kept on ice, it will keep up to five days in a cooler. In camps without refrigeration, hard-frozen meat will thaw nicely for the first night's dinner. But more than that is best left behind; it simply goes bad too fast.

In its place, campers can choose between old-fashioned, traditionally preserved meats (dried, salted, or smoked) and modern, industrially preserved ones (wet-cured, precooked, canned, or vacuum-packed). On most camping trips, the choice is not a difficult one to make. As far as good eating goes, tradition nearly always trumps the latest thing.

CURE-ALL: COUNTRY HAM

A weeklong fishing trip in Voyageurs National Park was delayed almost two days until we could find one. A sailboat trip to try our luck on the Bahamas Banks couldn't begin without one hanging in the galley. For two weeks at a camp in northwestern Ontario, one served us variously for breakfast, lunch, and dinner, yet never tasted the same way twice. It's an item that should always be on your outdoor grub list: country ham or, more precisely, country-cured ham.

There are three reasons why you don't want to go on a camping, hunting, or fishing trip without it.

NUMBER 1: NO OTHER MEAT KEEPS SO WELL, SO LONG, AND WITH SO LITTLE CARE IN THE FIELD.

That, indeed, is country ham's original and whole purpose. Before refrigeration, every frontier cabin or farm had a smokehouse hung heavy with ham and bacon. Hogs were easier, faster, and cheaper to raise than cattle (they could be fed almost anything or turned loose in the woods to fatten on nuts), which blessed pioneers with an abundance of pork—but cursed them with the problem of how to keep it all from going bad.

The ingenious "cure" was salt, woodsmoke, and time. Salt killed harmful bacteria, preventing spoilage, and also drew out moisture, reducing a ham's weight by 25 to 30 percent and, by happy coincidence, concentrating its natural flavor. Smoking drew out more moisture and added flavors and aromas of its own. Time—hanging the hams for four months to more than a year—added new dimensions of texture and taste. Hung from winter through spring, cold temperatures further dehydrated the ham, making the meat dense and compact. Left to hang all summer (through what old-time curemasters called the "summer sweat"), hot temperatures

Country Ham and Pastas, Soups, Stews

★

W hile country ham stands on its own, it is also the backbone of a number of hearty camp dishes. Slice it into slivers, panfry, and mix with red or white sauce and serve over pasta. Dice it and simmer with corn or beans to make a filling side dish. It makes a great extender of dehydrated soups. Chopped, tossed into a camp kettle and slow-cooked, with virtually whatever is on hand, it makes an authoritative stew that tastes singularly of natural ingredients, woodsmoke, and time well spent.

percolated fat, salt, and woodsmoke—and their flavors—throughout the meat.

As a result of this curing, country hams contain so little water that they can be safely stored without refrigeration for as long as you like—a boon on trips where there isn't any or ice chests are occupied. Just hang one in a shady corner of camp in its muslin sack and forget about it. It will supply all the meat you want, in delicious variety. It may, after a period, sport some patches of blue-gray mold on the outside, but not to worry. Just scrub it off; it's harmless. (In bear country, of course, all foods must be safely secured.)

NUMBER 2: NO OTHER MEAT IS MORE FLAVORFUL, AFIELD OR AFLOAT.

Country-cured ham is as exquisite and varied, flavorwise, as more expensive Italian prosciutto or Spanish serrano ham. The secret is in the all-American cures, which are as individual and imaginative as the curemasters themselves.

Try to find a locally cured ham wherever your next outing takes you. They're as distinctive as locally brewed beer or single-malt whiskeys, and well worth the time spent looking for them.

A plain, dry-cured ham—hand-rubbed with salt, left in a salt box for anywhere from two weeks to as long as 40 days, and then aged—is very good eating in itself. But a ham that has undergone a curemaster's art is gourmet fare in the field. Hams may be coated with cornmeal, black pepper, red pepper, or countless combinations of spices. Or they might be slathered with brown sugar, honey, molasses, or maple syrup, which not only sweetens the meat but also tenderizes it. Slowly smoking the hams—from 18 hours to as long as 14 days—over fruitwoods like apple or cherry; hardwoods like hickory, maple, or oak; or sometimes sassafras or even corn cobs adds a crowning touch. The meat takes on a sweet brown crust, a rich amber to deep mahogany color, a smoky taste, and a pungent aroma.

NUMBER 3: NO OTHER MEAT GOES FARTHER OUTDOORS.

Country ham is heavy, firm textured, intensely flavorful, and, yes, salty. In fact, it's like concentrated ham, so a little goes a long way. But as any camp cook can tell you, that's a good thing.

A whole ham (cut from the upper, meatiest part of a hog's hind leg) will easily outlast the appetites of large parties (six to eight people) on long trips (a week or more). Indeed, whole hams weigh from 12 to as much as 20 pounds, with 14 to 16 pounds a rough average, which is a lot of pork no matter how you slice it. According to the U.S. Department of Agriculture (your pork dollars at work), a bone-in country ham yields about one serving per three-quarters pound; a boneless country ham, about one serving per one-third pound. For camp use (unless you're planning to make soup with the hock), a boneless ham's the longer-eating, easier-to-work-with choice. A boneless middleweight (15-pound)

Country Ham and a Dram

★

My all-time favorite recipe for country ham in camp is by far the simplest. After a day's fishing, hunting, or paddling, while hungry campers are waiting for supper, it's also the most welcome.

Simply cut paper-thin slices of dry-cured ham (a fish fillet knife does this admirably). Serve atop thin-sliced rye, pumpernickel, or store-bought crispbread, with authoritative strong drink (see Chapter 18, "Big Medicine"). Whatever the evening meal, a libation will improve it— and the spirits of your party—immeasurably.

whole ham will provide 45 hefty servings; a boneless heavy-weight (20-pound) whole ham will furnish 60!

For smaller groups (four to six people) on shorter outings (four to five days), a half ham will furnish more than enough meat. A half ham generally weighs about 8 pounds and yields about 24 servings. A better choice may be a 5-pound picnic ham (cut from the hog's front shoulders).

For most of us—in parties of two to four, out for two or three days—vacuum-packed cuts of genuine country ham are the best way to go.

»»»» Grilled Country Ham Steaks ««««

Unless it's sliced thin, fried, or simmered in a soup or stew, country ham should be soaked in water before cooking. By law, country ham must have a salt content of at least 4 percent, which will pucker the taste buds if you don't soak some of it away. Once it is soaked, then basted with condiments common in camp and simply grilled, you will find it uncommonly good.

Serve with vegetables—potatoes, squash, corn—grilled over the same coals.

1 large country ham steak per person, cut 3/4 to
    1 inch thick
Honey, mustard, Worcestershire sauce, or other
    condiment for basting

Soak the steaks in a pot of cold water 4 hours or more. This is no hardship: put them in the water in the morning while you're frying ham and making gravy. To accelerate the process, change the water every hour or so.

When ready to cook, remove the steaks and slash the edges

(that way they'll lie flat instead of curling and will cook more evenly). Slather the steaks on both sides with your choice: honey, mustard (a mixture of the two is wonderful, too), maple syrup, or Worcestershire, soy, or barbecue sauce. Ham will take on the taste of whatever it's basted with. Place on a grill over medium-hot coals and grill 3 minutes a side. Turn the steaks once more, top with another coat of marinade, and grill until the coating glazes (2 to 3 minutes) or until it looks too good to resist. Note: In camps with ovens, broil in similar fashion on a rack, 3 inches from the heat.

>>>>> Cider-baked Country Ham <<<<<

Serves 6 to 8

This is definitely a dish reserved for large parties staying in an outpost or cabin with a reliable oven. It's an excellent way to prepare a half ham or what's left of a whole one after it's been used for camp breakfasts and dinners. Make sure everyone's darned hungry when you make it, however. It will feed six to eight campers an all-you-can-eat supper, with plenty of leftovers. Serve with cornbread, beans, and mustard greens.

    1 country-cured half ham (approximately 8 pounds)
    1 quart real apple cider (freeze-dried or powdered cider
        mixes work, too)
    4 or more whole cloves (weightless, and invaluable, in
        cooking ham)
    1/4 cup brown or maple sugar, or orange marmalade

Preheat the oven to 350°F. Place the ham in a large roasting pan, dish, or tin (anything big enough to hold it). Pour the cider over the ham, spike it with cloves, and cover with aluminum foil. Bake 3 to 3½ hours, or until done to taste. Remove from the oven and raise the temperature to 400° to 450°F. Baste the ham with the pan drippings and sprinkle with sugar or spread with marmalade. Return to the oven, uncovered, for 8 to 10 minutes, or until the outside of the ham is nicely glazed. Remove from the oven, let cool, and slice thin.

»»»» Canoeist's Ham-Apple-Cabbage «««««

Serves 4 to 6 paddlers

On one of the first long canoe trips I ever took, this dinner—made from outfitter-provided provisions—was a highlight. Not an ingredient in it requires refrigeration or gentle handling. The vacuum-packed ham steaks, generally ¼-inch center slices weighing 3/4 to 1 pound apiece, are "good to go" wherever and for as long as you're going. The same is true for the apples and cabbage. The dish is simply and easily made by even a greenhorn cook. Serve with a skillet of hot bannock.

4 tablespoons (½ stick) margarine
2 ham steaks, vacuum-packed (if cooking for 4, cut steaks in half)
1 cup freeze-dried apple cider (available at REI and other outdoor stores)
1 bouillon cube
2 medium red apples, cut in thin wedges (8 per apple)
1 small red cabbage, coarsely chopped
Salt and pepper
1 teaspoon dried thyme (optional, but very good)

Melt the margarine in a skillet and brown the ham steaks

well on both sides. Remove the meat leaving the drippings in the pan.

In a small bowl, mix the apple cider, 1 cup water, and the bouillon cube; add to the skillet with the pan drippings and stir. Lay the apple wedges in the bottom of the pan, cover with cabbage, and season with salt, pepper and thyme, if using. Place the ham on top. Cover and simmer for 15 to 20 minutes.

Bacon: Quintessential Camp Meat

If there's one emblematically paramount ingredient in American camp cooking, it is, oddly, the least American of all—bacon. Unlike corn, beans, squash, potatoes, turkey, and wild rice— indigenous American foods—hogs and their uninvited European owners arrived only a bit more than 500 years ago. While pigs were prized for their hams, it was the fat-rich meat from their bellies (bacon) that principally fuelled the newcomers' way west, mainly because—pound for pound—no other food packed more calories.

A pound of dry-cured bacon has nearly twice the calories of a pound of dry-cured ham. It has roughly two and a half times more calories than a pound of salted or dried beef. In fact, bacon has more calories (173 per ounce) than virtually anything else you can carry into the bush. The very few exceptions are butter or margarine (203 calories per ounce), pecans (195 calories per ounce), Brazil nuts (185 calories per ounce), and peanut butter (167 calories per ounce).

For generations of explorers, trappers, frontiersmen, pioneers, emigrants, prospectors, cowboys, loggers, hunters, and anglers—to whom maximum calories and long shelf life were life-and-death considerations—bacon was the mainstay. Dry-cured and smoked, much like the hams, it contained little water and lots of salt (6 to 7 percent by weight), and consequently kept well for months. More important, unlike hams, it was cheap and plentiful: the one meat everyone could afford.

But high calories, long shelf life, and low cost alone cannot account for bacon's legendary camp appeal. Bacon sizzling in a skillet is among the most revered icons in the panoply of American camp cooking—ranking with trout browning in a pan and "cowboy coffee" steeping in a pot. What distinguishes bacon—a high-fat (over 50 percent) and lowly cut of pork—is its phenomenal flavor. Renowned American chef James Beard called it "the most friendly of all meats, because it combines so freely and easily with other foods." To bard and baste lean venison, game birds, and fish, there's nothing finer. Combined with corn, beans, and potatoes—indeed, nearly any grain, vegetable, or green—it burnishes the flavors of its companions without overwhelming them. Its fat, poured off and saved in an old coffee tin, is ready-made frying oil or shortening.

Nowadays, of course, bacon has become something of public enemy number one, as far as health is concerned. It is, after all, fat from the fattest part of the fattest domesticated animal on earth. It's permeated with salt or brine. It contains both nitrates and nitrites which, at high cooking temperatures, combine to form nitrosamines, which may or may not be cancer-causing (current scientific opinion generally agrees the risk, if it exists, is small). Calorically, it's a Sumo wrestler.

On the other hand, three slices (approximately three ounces), panfried for breakfast, contain roughly 9 percent of an adult's recommended daily value (DV) of cholesterol, 15 percent of fat, and 20 percent of sodium. That's decidedly less of a menace (much less, in fact) than a drive-by, supersized burger, fries, and soft drink. Or a bucket of deep-fried chicken, mashed potatoes, and gravy. Or a carton of ice cream. In fact, it's a lot more benign than a three-ounce packet of instant ramen noodle soup, which contains 24 percent of an adult's DV of fat, 40 percent of saturated fat, and 74 percent of sodium.

FAKE BACON

Unfortunately, traditional dry-cured and smoked camp bacon is not as easy to find as it once was. Your supermarket may have it, packed in cotton sacks like country hams, so ask. Most times, however, you'll be pointed to an aisle-long display of modern, industrially wet-cured bacon. It is not the bacon you want. It is not bacon worth packing outdoors.

Because this product is wet, not dry-cured, it is—quite literally—filled with water. In fact, supermarket bacon is up to 66 percent water. That means it not only requires refrigeration, but will shrink to about one-third of its original weight once the water is cooked away. Indeed, after cooking, a pound of modern, wet-cured bacon will yield only about five ounces of meat. A pound of old-fashioned, dry-cured, smoked bacon, on the other hand, will yield about 12 ounces. The reason wet-cured bacon is so prevalent is simple economics: it's faster and thus cheaper to produce than dry-cured bacon. Instead of curing in a salt box for weeks, wet-cured bacon is factory-made in a day. The meat is stabbed with daggerlike arrays of needles, injected with a weak brine and sugar solution, and left to "age" for a couple hours. If it's labeled "smoked" or "smoke-cured," be assured it is not. It is lightly sprayed or washed with liquid flavorings that simulate smoke. Presliced, plastic-wrapped, and superabundant, however, it's the only bacon most Americans know.

In camp, wet-cured bacon is a nuisance. Unrefrigerated, it quickly goes bad. Fried, it evaporates. Its intact fat, unlike leaner, truly smoked bacon (rendered of a good portion of its fat), is prone to burn.

On your next camping trip, leave such fake bacon behind.

Take only the good old-fashioned dry-cured, unsliced variety. It will keep orders of magnitude longer, yield more than twice as much meat per pound, taste far better, and cook far more forgivingly. If you can't find it at your local supermarket, see the Camp Cook's Directory for sources (page 247).

»»»» Backpacker's Carbonara ««««

Serves 4

Genuine bacon is a camp cook's all-purpose meat. However it's prepared, it's good. With little effort, it can be sublime. Try this lightweight, old-time favorite on your next camping trip. It will feed four hungry hikers.

3 tablespoons olive oil
1/2 pound smoked bacon, diced
1/2 large onion, chopped
3 garlic cloves, chopped fine
2 cups dry red wine or water
3 large eggs
6 ounces hard cheese (Parmesan or Romano), grated
1 pound pasta
Salt and pepper

Put the oil, bacon, and onion in a frying pan, and heat over wood coals (or medium heat, if using a camp stove). Sauté, stirring, about 10 minutes, or until the bacon and onion are browned; add the garlic and cook for a minute longer. Add the wine to the pan, simmer for 5 minutes, and keep warm. Meanwhile, bring a large pot of water to a boil for the pasta. Mix the eggs and cheese in a bowl and set aside.

Add the pasta to the boiling water and cook 8 to 10 minutes. Drain. Pour the egg mixture over the pasta and stir well. Then pour the bacon mixture over the pasta and stir well. Season with salt and pepper and serve.

CURED SAUSAGES

In the category of no-cook, ready-to-eat camp meats that keep virtually indefinitely, cured sausages stand paramount. High in protein, fat, and flavor, they're perfect for lunches and snacks. They're also wonderful in camp-made sauces, soups, and stews. There are thousands of varieties. Among those commonly found in supermarkets are a few that the smart camp cook should always include on the grub list.

Genoa salami—a hard, dry Italian sausage seasoned with peppercorns and garlic—will taste great and keep wonderfully for weeks. *Jaeger* (German for hunter)—a dried, smoked sausage of beef and pork—will do likewise. So will dried Spanish chorizo—a coarse-cut pork sausage seasoned with paprika. Dried, highly seasoned Polish kielbasa is another flavorful, long-keeping choice for campers. Smoked Italian link sausage, made from coarse-ground pork, either mildly or hotly seasoned, needs to be briefly boiled or browned before eating but can be safely carried for a week.

FRESH SAUSAGE

Fresh ground sausage is wonderful camp food—as long as you've got an ice chest or refrigerator in camp. For food safety's sake, it should always be refrigerated or frozen. That doesn't mean you have to leave it behind on backpacking trips: fresh sausage makes a superlative first-night supper. Hard frozen at home before you hit the trail, it will keep quite well until you make camp. Most people mix it with either dried or canned tomato sauce to make spaghetti sauce.

Personally, I think it's much better cooked with rice. One pound of ground pork sausage, combined with a half-pound of yellow rice (which is preseasoned), is spicy, quick, and simple to prepare (even on a one-burner camp stove), and will easily feed four.

›››› Camper's Dirty Rice ‹‹‹‹

You don't really need to serve anything alongside this dish. It's full-flavored and filling enough on its own, but any kind of salad or slaw would go well with it. Yellow rice is preseasoned, so you don't have to add anything.

One 8-ounce packet yellow rice
3 garlic cloves, chopped
1 pound fresh ground pork sausage (available mild, medium, or hot)
Pepper and Tabasco

In the 2-quart pot of your cook kit, boil water, add the rice, and simmer according to package instructions (generally 15 to 20 minutes). Drain, cover, and set aside. Put the garlic and sausage in a frying pan. Fry over medium heat, stirring occasionally, for 6 to 8 minutes or until the sausage is well crumbled and browned (none of the meat should be pink). Empty the sausage—grease and all—into the rice and mix well. Season with pepper and Tabasco sauce to taste.

★ CHAPTER 9 ★

FISHY BUSINESS

The Finest Outdoor Eating

I have laid aside business, and gone a-fishing.

—IZAAK WALTON, 1653

FOR THREE days in the summer of 1959, my family was rainbound in an Adirondack lean-to at Marcy Lake. As a kid, I thought we ate well: instant oatmeal with raisins and brown sugar, milk biscuits spread with peanut butter, pork and beans with slices of fried Spam. That changed the evening a solitary hiker carrying a pack, rod case, and stringer of jewel-bright trout appeared out of the rain. We made room for him in the shelter and he was soon frying the fish—small ones, with the heads still on—in a skillet with bacon. He ate them with his fingers, like corn on the cob, smiling the whole time.

»»»» Perfect Panfried Trout ««««

Serves 2

If there's any dish in American camp cooking finer than a sublime mess of fresh-caught trout sizzling in a skillet, I don't know what it is. A Who's Who of American anglers have waxed eloquent about it, from Henry David Thoreau and Teddy Roosevelt to Dwight Eisenhower and Ted Williams, to name but a few. But angling authority A. J. McClane perhaps put it best: "Purists will agree that pan-fried trout cooked at streamside is a culinary superlative, assuming, of course, that the chef has mastered this basic skill."

The skill isn't hard to learn. Mastering its many permutations may take longer. But the beginner can't go far wrong following this basic recipe.

1/2 cup cornmeal or flour
2 whole trout (gilled and gutted)
1/4 cup vegetable oil
Salt and pepper
Melted butter and fresh lemon wedges for serving

Put the cornmeal or flour in a brown paper bag, drop in the trout, and shake until the fish are nicely coated. (Or put the cornmeal on a plate and dredge fish in it.)

Set a skillet over glowing wood coals (medium heat if you're using a camp stove) and heat the oil 2 to 3 minutes or until hot enough that water dropped into it sizzles.

The heat of the oil, as much as the freshness of the fish, is the key to perfect panfried trout. The hotter, the better, which is why butter and bacon grease, prone to smoking at comparatively low temperatures, are better suited for other culinary exploits. Vegetable oils (corn, peanut, cottonseed, or safflower) all have a comparatively high smoking point, ideal for searing and cooking fish.

Lay the coated trout in the oiled skillet. Fry 3 to 4 minutes on one side; turn and fry 2 to 3 minutes on the other side. When the trout is crisply browned, stick a fork into it and twist. If the flesh flakes easily from the bones, it's done. Remove from heat, dab the fish with butter, squirt with fresh lemon juice, and serve.

»»»» Panfried Trout Saussignac ««««

(from Frederick Montayne, Chateau Saussignac.)

Serves 2

A dog-eared copy of this recipe was found tacked to the wall of a fishing cabin on Fightingtown Creek in the southern Appalachians. I'm grateful to whoever left it there and, of course, to Monsieur Montayne. I've used it for many years. It makes a superlative trout.

2 tablespoons butter or margarine
$1/4$ cup chopped hazelnuts
2 whole trout (gilled and gutted)
2 tablespoons fresh sorrel leaves (found in the herb
    section of your supermarket)
1 tablespoon vegetable oil

In a skillet, melt 1 tablespoon of the butter over medium heat. Add the hazelnuts and cook 1 to 2 minutes, or until lightly browned, stirring constantly. Remove the nuts and set aside.

Stuff the cavity of each trout with 1 tablespoon of sorrel

leaves. Wipe out the skillet and heat the remaining 1 table-spoon of butter and the oil over medium heat, until the butter melts. Lay the trout in the skillet. Panfry for 6 to 8 minutes, or until the fish are golden brown. Before serving, sprinkle evenly with hazelnuts.

Simply done and simply delicious.

»»» Trout Hemingway «««

Serves 1

If you'd like to fry trout "Papa's" way, here's how he explained it in a newspaper dispatch in the *Toronto Star* in the 1920s. Be careful it doesn't burn, as this method involves frying in hot bacon grease. And be sure you like your trout bacon-flavored, because it will be.

3 slices bacon
1 whole trout (gilled and gutted)
Cornmeal (to coat fish)

The method—in Hemingway's own words—is as concise as the ingredients: "The proper way is to cook over coals. Put the bacon in [a frying pan] and when it is about half cooked, lay the trout in the hot grease, dipping them in cornmeal first. Then put the bacon on top of the trout and it will baste them as it slowly cooks."

>>>>> Cornmeal-fried Catfish <<<<<

Serves 4

This all-American dish is a traditional favorite in fish camps from the lower Mississippi to the upper Missouri—anywhere "cats" and cornmeal are found. But the recipe works quite as well with almost any filleted fish. Served with hush puppies (recipe follows), creamy coleslaw, and ice-cold beer, it's great eating.

1 cup cornmeal, white or yellow (or combine $1/2$ cup of each)
1 tablespoon salt
1 tablespoon pepper
2 large eggs, beaten
4 catfish fillets (about $1/2$ pound each)
1 cup vegetable oil

In a brown paper bag, mix the cornmeal, salt, and pepper (if you don't have a bag, mix them on a plate). In bowl, beat the eggs with 2 tablespoons of water. Dip the fillets in the egg and water mix, drop them into the bag and shake until coated (or dredge them in the cornmeal on the plate).

In an iron skillet, heat the oil until spitting—but not smoking—hot. Fry the fillets 5 to 8 minutes, turning once, until golden brown. Serve immediately.

››››› Hush Puppies ‹‹‹‹‹

Serves 4 (makes 12 to 16 hush puppies)

There is, in my piscine experience, no finer accompaniment to fresh-caught fish than the humble hush puppy. Not only do these fried, doughy nuggets taste out of this world, but the fixings are lightweight and—serendipitously—a subset of the ingredients needed to panfry a shore lunch anyway.

Don't, by any means, let what appears to be a longish list of ingredients convince you this simple side dish is too much trouble to take afield. The dry ingredients and oil, spooned into two zip-lock bags, can be carried in the pocket of a pair of fatigue pants. So, too, can the small onion and tin of creamed corn. The lone egg, well wrapped in a bandanna or paper towels, is best carried on your head, under your hat. Don't laugh. It's positive insurance it will arrive intact.

1 cup yellow cornmeal
$\frac{1}{3}$ cup self-rising flour or Bisquick
1 tablespoon brown sugar
1 large egg
$\frac{1}{4}$ cup finely chopped onion
One 8-ounce can creamed corn
$\frac{1}{4}$ cup fresh or dried milk (buttermilk is best)
1 to 2 cups vegetable oil (1 to 2 inches deep) for frying

In a bowl, mix the cornmeal, flour, and sugar. Add the egg, onion, corn, and milk and stir to make a stiff batter.

In an iron skillet, heat the oil until sputtering hot. Drop the batter by heaping tablespoons into the hot oil. Don't crowd the pan: fry a few at a time, for 4 to 5 minutes, or until deep brown. Drain on a paper-towel-covered plate, if possible, and keep warm (in an oven or fireside) while you fry the fish.

»»»» Mini Fish Fry ««««

Serves 2

Good fishing waters usually sport teeming populations of minnows and various baitfish. Most fishing camps, in fact, are hung like Christmas trees with assorted minnow traps, scoops, and casting nets.

Many anglers, however, fail to appreciate that the small fry that trout, walleye, and bass delight in eating make equally delightful eating for people. I certainly did, until shown otherwise by a French Canadian. On an otherwise fishless afternoon, he waded into the lake shallows and netted a quantity of small, silvery ciscoes—not for bait, but to make what he called an *amuse-gueule* (cocktail snack).

Minnows are too small to gut and clean with a knife, of course. By hand, however, it's easily done. Just grasp the minnow between your forefinger and thumb—do this over some outspread newspaper—and gently squeeze its underbelly with your thumb. The guts will come out through the hole (anal vent) in its abdomen. The process, rather like squeezing seeds from a grape, leaves the flesh intact. There's no need to worry about removing the minuscule bones or head; the cooking will render them perfectly edible.

1 pound cleaned minnows (ciscoes, roaches, smelts, etc.)
2 tablespoons salt
1½ cups milk
1½ cups self-rising flour or Bisquick
Vegetable oil for frying

Put the minnows in a saucepan, add the salt and milk, and let soak for 15 to 20 minutes. Put the flour in a brown paper bag. Drain minnows, drop them into the bag, and shake until coated. Heat vegetable oil to a depth of 1 to 2 inches until

TABLEWORTHY SCRAPS

★

Don't be too quick about surrendering your fish scraps to the herons or gulls. As these birds know only too well, there's usually a fair amount of meat left on a fish after filleting. Keep these choice, richly flavored morsels for yourself and your camp mates.

Once you've removed the fillets, cut the guts, gills, fins, and tail from the carcass and discard (the birds will be quite happy with these). Then chop off the head and section the remainder of the carcass into convenient pieces. Put these pieces (the head, too) into a pot with enough water to cover. Over medium heat, bring to a boil, then reduce the heat and simmer for half an hour. That's it.

Flake the meat from the head and bones with a fork and use for fish cakes. The flavor-filled pot water (or fish stock, prized by chefs)—strained through a sieve or a clean bandanna to catch any loose bones—makes exquisitely tasty soups or chowders.

hot enough to sputter. Fry the minnows a handful at a time to golden crispness, like French fries. Serve piping hot, well salted, with cocktails or cold beer.

»»» Sautéed and Brandied Pike ««««

Serves 4 (in civilization) or 2 (in the bush)

At first, Northern pike's a difficult fish to like. It's ugly, bony, and has a mouthful of long, recurved, needle-sharp teeth. A 20-million-year-old predator, it lies in ambush, strikes with fury, and devours whatever it can swallow: fish, frogs, mice, muskrats, and, especially, ducklings. Hooked and boated, it's no friendlier. Cleaning one for the table's a pain, because pike have a hedgehog of pesky Y-shaped bones just above the rib cage. Removing them (while pestered by yellowjackets or biting flies) takes some patience and the sacrifice of a portion of the fillet. Most anglers don't bother and throw back any pike they catch. In doing so, they throw away some fine eating.

The secret to liking pike is getting someone else to clean them. The way to do this is to volunteer to cook the danged things. This strategy has worked for me for 20 years and results in effortlessly cleaned (for the cook, anyway), bone-free pike fillets. Because the meat is lean, it's best panfried, deep-fried, broiled, or baked. This recipe's a favorite, until the brandy runs out.

1 cup milk
1 large egg, beaten
1/2 cup crushed potato chips (remains from lunch)
1 cup crushed cornflakes (remains from breakfast)
1 1/2 pounds Northern pike, filleted (about 1/2 inch thick)
4 to 6 tablespoons butter

2 apples or oranges, sliced thin

$\frac{1}{4}$ cup brandy

In a bowl, mix the milk and egg. Combine the potato chips and cornflakes on a plate. Dip the fillets in the milk-egg mixture, then coat with the potato chips and cornflakes.

In a large iron skillet, melt the butter. Add the fillets and apple slices (if using orange slices, squeeze them over the fish first and toss in the pulpy rinds) and sauté over medium heat for about 3 minutes, or until the fish is lightly browned on one side. Turn and sauté $1\frac{1}{2}$ to 3 minutes more, until the other side is golden brown. Remove from heat, pour in the brandy, and light it with a match.

Watch its low, blue flame burn out and serve the fillets immediately, topped with the sautéed fruit and butter-brandy mixture from the pan.

»»»» Sautéed Walleye with Wild Rice «««« and Mushrooms

Serves 4

Nobody loves this dorsal-sailed, iridescent, bug-eyed fish for its looks. Everybody, however, loves its firm, sweet, tasty meat. Indeed, most anglers agree that walleye is the tastiest of all freshwater North American game fish.

It's equally fine fried, broiled, baked, or boiled. This Canadian fish camp version is particularly good and makes a good-looking presentation, too.

2 ounces dried mushrooms (morels, shiitake, or porcini)

3 cups cooked wild rice (see page 226 for how to cook wild rice)

6 tablespoons butter or margarine
2 pounds walleye, filleted (about $\frac{1}{2}$ inch thick)
Salt and pepper
Lemon wedges

Soak the dried mushrooms in a bowl of hot water for 30 minutes or until soft. Drain and set aside. Keep the cooked rice warm in an oven set at low heat (about 140°F).

Melt 3 tablespoons of the butter in a skillet over medium heat. Add the mushrooms and, stirring constantly, sauté about 5 minutes or until gently browned. Remove from the pan to keep warm.

Over medium heat, melt the remaining butter in the skillet. Add the fillets and sauté about 3 minutes on each side, turning once, until golden brown. Remove from heat.

On a big platter, dish out the wild rice, artfully arrange the fillets on top, adorn with mushrooms, salt and pepper the whole affair, and ring the platter with fresh-cut lemon wedges.

»»» Beer-battered Smallmouth «««

Serves 2

Despite their diminutive size (two to three pounds, on average), these olive-gold, bronze-tinted fish were called *achigan,* or ferocious, by the Algonquian. Few freshwater fishes fight harder or more acrobatically. Few are finer in the pan. Old-fashioned beer batter is good for frying any fish, of course, but it's especially good enfolding a tendersweet "smallie."

1 cup all-purpose flour or Bisquick
$\frac{1}{2}$ bottle of beer (6 ounces)
2 large eggs

1 tablespoon vegetable oil, plus more for sautéing
1/2 teaspoon each salt and pepper
2 pounds smallmouth fillets
Bread or cracker crumbs, flour, or cornmeal (to coat
  the fish)

In a bowl, mix the flour, beer, eggs, oil, salt, and pepper to the consistency of pancake batter. Drop the fillets in the batter and let sit there 1 or 2 minutes. Place the bread crumbs on a plate and dredge the fillets to coat. Heat 1/4 cup of oil in a skillet and fry the fish until golden brown on both sides.

»»»» Blackened Yellow Perch ««««

Serves 4

Called the striped or convict perch because of the black stripes lining its yellow body, this is arguably the most popular panfish in America, primarily because it is abundant, easily caught, and great eating. Though they're small (usually no more than a pound), perch move in schools and bite willingly, so where one is taken an angler can quickly secure a half-dozen or more.

They're delicious panfried plain, flour-coated, or dipped in batter, but blackened perch are something else. You can find plenty of premade blackening mixes at your grocery store, all of which are quite good. Or you can just as easily buy the spices yourself, jangle them all together in a big zip-lock bag, and tote your homemade concoction to camp. In fact, you probably won't have to buy most of the seasonings. They're likely sitting in your pantry at home already.

8 tablespoons (1 stick) butter
5 tablespoons paprika

1 tablespoon chili powder

2 teaspoons onion powder

1 teaspoon thyme

1 teaspoon oregano

1 teaspoon white pepper

1 teaspoon black pepper

1 teaspoon cayenne

1 teaspoon salt

2 to 3 pounds whole perch, gilled and gutted (leave
heads on)

1/2 cup vegetable oil (peanut oil works best)

Melt the butter in an iron skillet, and pour it into a bowl. Combine all the seasonings in a small bowl. Dip the perch in the butter. Rub with blackening mix to coat. Over hot coals, heat the vegetable oil in the same skillet.

Carefully lay the fish in the skillet and stand back. They'll hiss and smoke like the devil. Cook 2 to 4 minutes, turning the fish every minute, until they're blackened on the outside and a fork shows them flaky white on the inside.

»»»» Simple Fish Fingers ««««

"Simplify" was one of Thoreau's guiding principles. So far as cooking the day's catch goes, there's nothing simpler than this tried-and-true recipe. All you need is some steak sauce (Worcestershire, A.1., Heinz 57) and good old Bisquick. It's quite as good as anything fancier. Serve with lemon wedges, green salad, and plenty of tartar sauce.

Filleted fish (any kind), cut into strips

Steak sauce

Bisquick, pancake mix, or self-rising flour

½ cup vegetable oil for frying

Lay the fish strips on a plate, cover with steak sauce, and let marinate 1 hour. Heat the oil in a skillet. Put some Bisquick in a brown paper bag. Drop the strips into the bag, shake until coated, and fry in hot oil until brown and crisp.

»»»» North Woods Fish Boil ««««

Serves 4

I love fried fish, but not every day. Unfortunately, that's pretty much how it's always prepared in fish camps.

Ironically, the traditional way to prepare fish in the North Woods was to boil it. That's how the Indian nations did it, and the voyageurs, trappers, prospectors, and loggers imitated their method. It was simple (boil a kettle of water), easy (toss in fresh or dried vegetables and steaked fish), and quick (a half hour's boil)—the original one-pot meal. It was economical: the oily fish used (lake trout and salmon) were abundant, easily caught, and free, and substituted quite handsomely for harder-to-get, laboriously rendered, and expensive animal fats (bear oil in the Indian days, imported salt pork or fatback with the arrival of Europeans). What's more—and I suspect the real reason why the "fish boil" has been a Great Lakes staple for centuries—it's a bracing, wonderfully filling alternative to fried fish in camp.

4 medium potatoes, unpeeled

4 medium onions, whole (skins removed)

4 carrots, sliced

¼ cup salt

2 pounds fish steaks (1 inch thick)

Bring a big pot of water (4 quarts) to a rolling boil. Add the potatoes, onions, carrots, and salt; return to a boil and partially cover. Boil 15 to 18 minutes, or until the potatoes are easily pierced by a fork. Drop in the fish steaks, partially cover, and boil another 10 to 12 minutes, or until the fish flakes with a twist of a fork. Drain the fish and vegetables and serve piping hot.

>>>>> Pickerel Stew <<<<<

(Adopted from Grace Mullner, Friends of the Atikokan Centennial Museum)

Serves 4

For almost 20 years, I've outfitted out of a little town in the lake country of northwestern Ontario called Atikokan (which means "caribou bones" in Ojibway). Sitting between the Quetico/ Boundary Waters Wilderness to the south and the White Otter Wilderness to the north, it's a perfect jumping-off place for canoeists and anglers, as well as home to some of the friendliest folks I've ever met.

When it comes to cooking in the bush, they can make even a common pickerel (a small one, at that) into a warming, memorable meal.

1 pound pickerel fillets
6 slices bacon, diced
2 tablespoons butter
1 onion, diced
$^{1}/_{2}$ cup chopped celery
2 cups diced potatoes
$^{1}/_{2}$ cup chopped carrots
1 tomato, chopped

1 teaspoon salt

$^1/_2$ teaspoon pepper

One 10-ounce can evaporated milk

Cut the fillets into bite-size pieces.

In a large skillet, fry the bacon, drain, and set aside. In the same skillet, melt the butter, add the onion and celery, and sauté over medium heat until the onion is translucent. Transfer the onion and celery to a 2-quart pot. Add the potatoes, carrots, tomato, salt, pepper, bacon, and 2 cups of water. Cover, bring to a boil, and simmer for 20 minutes or until the vegetables are tender. Add the fish and simmer another 10 minutes. Add the milk and reheat, but do not boil.

A Surefire Shore Lunch

Among the mind-boggling number of "traditional" shore lunch menus, two stand out. Both, despite similarities, are quite different in terms of ingredients, method, and cooking time. One is artistic, an epitome of outdoor cookcraft, in fact; the other is simplistic, but oddly, just as good.

The Thousand Islands shore lunch, cooked up by fishing guides on the U.S.–Canada border along the upper St. Lawrence River in the 1890s, is legendary. The classic menu commences with fried fatback (never bacon) and onion sandwiches, accompanied by a green salad with homemade Thousand Island dressing (and only Thousand Island dressing). The main course consists of parboiled potatoes and flour-coated fresh fish (smallmouth bass only), deep fried in fatback grease (never vegetable oil). Batter-dipped French toast, deep fried in the same grease, and crowned with equal capfuls of heavy cream, maple syrup, and brandy, makes dessert.

Whipping this up in the wild—as any guide will tell

you—isn't easy. It involves packing a lot of perishables (salad greens, mayonnaise, cream, store-bought bread), a lot of prep time (frying out fatback, boiling potatoes), and a short-order cook's skill to make it all come out right and in sequence. That's why other than on guided trips (where it costs an angler $15)—it remains a delicacy.

The bush shore lunch, a North Woods tradition in its own right, is a far quicker, easier, and more economical alternative, especially on camping-fishing trips without benefit of refrigeration, ice, or guide-cooks. In fact, for do-it-yourself camp cooks—like most of us—it's foolproof. Ironically, except for the fish, none of the ingredients is fresh. This, of course, directly contradicts most of what this book recommends. No matter. All rules, on occasion, merit breaking.

For surely and safely turning potatoes and fish in hot oil, tongs are far better than a spatula. A long-handled metal spoon is better for stirring hot cans of beans and corn than a short-handled one. Gloves, which most anglers carry anyway, make working close to a hot grill much more pleasant. Using two big skillets (one for potatoes, one for fish) will speed things up considerably and assure both are served piping hot.

››››› Shore Lunch Bush-style ‹‹‹‹‹

Serves 6

One 16-ounce can pork and beans
One 16-ounce can corn
1 quart vegetable oil
One 16-ounce can whole potatoes
3 pounds fresh-caught fish, filleted
2 cups flour or cornmeal (or a mixture)

Open the cans of pork and beans and corn, leaving the lids partially attached (they'll give you something to grip as you stir the contents while cooking). Set them on a grill over glowing coals, and watch the labels burn off (it's fun and you can bet on which burns off first).

Fill a large skillet 2 inches deep with vegetable oil and heat until it is bubbling hot (which takes a fraction of the time, fuel, and trouble of rendering fatback). Drain the potatoes (they're already parboiled, eliminating 30 minutes or more of cooking time). Drop them (carefully) into the hot oil and fry.

As the potatoes brown, cut the fish into cubes. Put the flour in a brown paper bag, drop the fish into the bag, and shake to coat.

When the potatoes are nicely browned (5 to 7 minutes), remove them from the skillet, drain on paper towels, and set aside. Drop the fish cubes (a handful at a time) into the hot oil. Fry 2 to 3 minutes, turning occasionally, until they are golden brown. They will float to the surface when they're done. Remove, drain on paper towels, cover, and set near the grill to keep warm while you fry the rest (refreshing the oil as needed).

Let each angler spoon a portion of pork and beans, corn, fried potatoes, and crispy fresh fish.

››››› In Lieu of Fresh Fish ‹‹‹‹‹

Serves 1

All anglers fail occasionally or—more honestly—oftener than they'll admit. I suppose that's why canned sardines, packed in olive oil, are a time-honored outdoor staple. They're rich in fat, protein, and calories.

Usually they're eaten straight out of the can or mashed between bread or crackers. But they're just as easy—and far better—fried. Lacking fresh fish for a shore lunch, try this way of sprucing up sardines. You'll never eat them cold out of a can again.

1 tin sardines, packed in olive oil
1 lemon wedge

Empty the sardines and their oil into a small skillet (a mess tin plate will do). Fry over a fistful of twigs, stirring, until crispy brown. Squirt with lemon and eat hot.

PART V

Soups and Stews

★ CHAPTER 10 ★

THE MISSING COURSE

Soup is, or should be, a leading food element in
every woodland camp.

—NESSMUK (GEORGE W. SEARS), 1920

N O **EXPERIENCED** camper ventures far afield without toting at least one pair of dry socks. It's just common sense. Oddly, few tote its culinary equivalent: soup.

In general, nothing is more rehydrating, warming, and welcome in camp than hot soup. In a wet camp, it's salvation.

The only real question for the camp cook is whether to pack prepared soup or make it from scratch. There is, of course, a world of difference between the two. Choosing one over the other depends entirely upon the world in which they must be made.

Prepared Soups

On backpacking and canoe trips, fresh soups are best made on layover days, when a slow-simmering pot causes no complaint. On other days, lacking the time, fuel, or patience for cooking, prepared soups will have to do. Instant soups—the add-boiling-water-and-eat variety—are hardly epicurean, but in a cold drizzle there's nothing quicker.

The downside—as in all condensed and instant soups—is the salt. For adults, the recommended daily allowance of sodium is 2,300 milligrams, or about one teaspoon of salt a day. A cup of instant (dried) chicken noodle soup contains 720 milligrams, or roughly one-third of a day's sodium in a food that contains only a twentieth of a day's calories. A cup of condensed (canned) tomato soup contains 744 milligrams. A cup of condensed (canned) beef noodle soup contains 952 milligrams. A diminutive cube of beef bouillon (typically 6 grams or somewhat less than a tablespoon) contains a whopping 1,019 milligrams.

As a general practice, I tuck a few packets of instant soup into the cook kit for use when there's no time for anything else. But I also pack select dehydrated, organic (natural) soups (see a partial listing in the Camp Cook's Directory, page 247). These are three to four times heavier than instant soups, as they contain whole, dried vegetables and other ingredients rather than powdered or hydrolyzed ones. Consequently, they take longer to cook—about 20 minutes of simmering—but they are, unequivocally, worth waiting for. Their texture, taste, and nutritive value—dried organic soups retain almost 95 percent of their natural nutrients—rival those of fresh homemade soups. Better yet, they are not only additive-free, but contain from 50 to 70 percent *less* sodium than instant and condensed varieties.

CAMP-MADE SOUPS

Freshly made soup—infinitely better than anything store-bought—takes time, but is surprisingly little trouble. In fact, in inclement weather, in base camps, cabins, or cottages, it's great fun. Rained out from other activities, luxuriating in your last pair of dry socks, there is no finer way to invest your time.

»»»» McQuat Lake Potato Soup «««

Serves 4 generously

For three consecutive days of unending rain in the Canadian bush, my partner and I were confined in a half-century-old log cabin. The roof leaked, puddles covered the warped plank floor, and it seemed darker and wetter inside than out. This simple soup, substantial, easy, and quick to make, soothed our soaked spirits. We practically lived on it until the skies cleared.

4 medium potatoes, diced
2 celery ribs, chopped
2 carrots, chopped
1 medium onion, chopped
2 garlic cloves, minced
Salt and pepper
1 cup milk
4 tablespoons ($^1\!/_2$ stick) butter, plus more for serving
2 slices cooked bacon, crumbled, for serving (left-over from breakfast)
Dark rye or pumpernickel bread

Put the vegetables, garlic, salt, and pepper into a soup pot or camp kettle, and add enough water to cover (3 or 4 cups). Bring to a boil, then simmer, covered, for 20 to 25 minutes or until the veggies are tender. Stir in the milk and coarsely mash the veggies with a potato masher or fish club: four or five murderous strokes, no more; it is best chunky. Add the butter and heat to serving temperature, about as long as it takes for the butter to melt. Garnish with the bacon. Serve with thin slices of dark rye or pumpernickel breads (both of which keep well) and butter.

>>>>> Lentil Soup with Dumplings <<<<<

Serves 4

The ingredients required to make this filling, old-time camp favorite consist of lightweight, low-volume, long-keeping staples. Cooking takes no more than about an hour.

4 slices bacon, diced
2 garlic cloves, minced
1 small onion, chopped
1 carrot, chopped
$1/2$ pound lentils
1 cup Bisquick or all-purpose flour

In a skillet, fry the bacon and garlic until just browned. Transfer to a soup pot; add the onion, carrot, and lentils and about 3 cups water, or enough to cover the lentils. Bring to a boil; reduce the heat, cover, and simmer for 30 to 45 minutes, or until the lentils are tender. If making dumplings, add them after the lentils have cooked 20 to 30 minutes.

For dumplings, mix 1 cup Bisquick and $1/4$ cup water in a

bowl, and stir into a stiff batter. Drop tablespoons of batter into the soup, cover, and let steam for the last 15 to 20 minutes of cooking time. Serve when the dumplings are cooked through.

›››› Deer Shack Soup ‹‹‹‹

Serves 4

The best fare to revive a chilled, dehydrated, luckless party of hunters is this soup or any of a thousand equally good variations of it. It's easy and relatively quick to prepare (an hour or so), but much better when allowed to simmer longer. Serve with hot bannock (see page 102) for dipping in the broth.

1 cup cornmeal
1 pound stew beef, in chunks
2 tablespoons vegetable oil
4 large potatoes, cubed
2 medium onions, chopped
4 celery ribs, chopped
Salt and pepper

Put the cornmeal in a brown paper bag, add the beef, and shake until coated. In a cast-iron skillet, heat the oil, add the beef, and sauté until well browned (8 to 10 minutes). Drain on paper towels and set aside.

In a large pot, bring 2 quarts of water to a rolling boil. Add the potatoes, onions, and celery, cover, and simmer over medium heat for about 20 minutes or until the vegetables are tender. Add the beef and stir in salt and pepper to taste; cover and simmer for 20 to 25 minutes, stirring occasionally. Serve in bowls.

››››› Paddlers Pea Soup ‹‹‹‹‹

Serves 4 to 6

The legendary French-Canadian voyageurs subsisted on a more basic variation of this dish and never tired of it. On camping trips without refrigeration, this slightly updated version works just as well. The bouillon and smoked ham make it flavorfully, but sensibly, salty (about 300 milligrams per serving). Serve with biscuits or dumplings.

1 cup dried split peas
2 bay leaves (optional)
2 medium carrots, minced
1 medium onion, chopped
1 bouillon cube (beef, chicken, or vegetable)
2 garlic cloves, minced
1 cup diced cured, smoked ham
Pepper

Bring the peas and 4 cups water to a boil in a large pot. Parboil the peas for 2 minutes, then let stand 1 hour (see page 184). Don't drain; the water is filled with nutrients and flavor and shouldn't be discarded. Add the bay leaves, if using, the carrots, onion, bouillon, garlic, and ham. Stir, cover, and simmer over medium heat for about 45 minutes or until the peas have disintegrated. Remove the bay leaves; add pepper to taste, stir, and simmer, uncovered, for 5 to 7 minutes. If the soup is too thick, thin with water to desired consistency. Serve hot.

›››› Corn Soup ‹‹‹‹

Serves 4

Traditionally, this Native American camp favorite was made with fresh or parched (dried) corn. Today, freeze-dried corn (one of the few freeze-dried foods almost equal in taste and texture to its fresh equivalent) substitutes admirably for campers. Canned whole-kernel corn is a cheaper, more expedient, choice. The milk can be either fresh, evaporated, UHT/retort-packaged, or reconstituted dried.

1/2 pound salt pork, chopped fine
2 large onions, sliced
3 medium potatoes, diced
2 cups fresh corn (from 4 ears) or 1 packet (1 1/2 ounces)
    freeze-dried
1 cup milk
2 tablespoons butter
Salt and pepper

In a large soup pot, fry the salt pork until browned. Add the onions and sauté about 5 minutes or until translucent. Add 4 cups water, the potatoes, and corn. (If you're using fresh corn, be sure to scrape the milk from the cobs into the pot: the sweet liquor and fleshy fragments are wonderfully tasty.) Bring to a boil, reduce the heat, and simmer for a half hour. Stir in the milk, butter, and salt and pepper to taste. Heat to serving temperature, being careful not to boil it.

>>>>> Camp-style Bean Soup <<<<<

Serves 4

Homemade bean soup is camp soul food. The soul derives from using whole, unadulterated, dried beans, which—like anything soulful—require time. They must be soaked overnight or parboiled, which isn't nearly as troublesome as it sounds (see Chapter 12: "You Don't Know Beans"). The result—nearly everyone's favorite outdoor soup—is well worth it.

2 cups dried beans (Great Northern or navy beans are
   best)
2 medium potatoes, diced
1 medium onion, diced
4 garlic cloves, minced
One 4-ounce can tomato paste (optional)
$1/4$ pound salt pork, chopped fine
Pepper

Either presoak or parboil the beans in a large pot (see page 184). (If presoaking, drain and add 4 cups water prior to cooking; if parboiling, retain the 4 cups of water in which they were boiled.) Add the potatoes, onion, garlic, and tomato paste (if using) to the beans. Stir, bring to a boil, and simmer 1 hour.

While the soup is simmering, brown the salt pork in a skillet, add to the pot, and stir. Add pepper to taste (the pork has plenty of salt). Stir and taste occasionally; serve when the beans are tender.

Quick Camp Squash Soup

Serves 4

Making soup from a vegetable as big as a squash usually intimidates campers. They think hours of prep work and simmering are somehow mandatory. That's not the case with this easily made and fast-cooking camp soup. If you can chop vegetables and boil water, you can confidently make this dish.

Use acorn or butternut for a rich orange-colored soup. Cut the squash in half and seed. Then place the halves face down on a cutting board, cut into wedges about $1/2$ inch thick, turn the wedges on their sides, and slice off the rind. Cut the peeled squash into $1/2$-inch cubes.

4 cups chicken stock or water
1 large butternut squash or 2 medium acorn squash, cubed
4 shallots, chopped (chopped onion or scallions may be substituted)
1 cup milk (or half-and-half or cream, if you can spare it)
$1/4$ cup brown sugar (or maple syrup or honey)
1 tablespoon salt
1 tablespoon pepper
Cinnamon or nutmeg

In a large pot, combine the stock, squash, shallots, milk, and sugar. Over medium heat, bring to a boil; reduce the heat and simmer for 8 to 10 minutes or until the squash is tender. Remove the pot from heat, add salt and pepper, and mash the vegetables evenly. Then (with a spoon, fork, or whisk) whip the mixture thoroughly until creamy.

Return the pot to low heat and simmer, stirring, until piping hot. Serve with a sprinkling of cinnamon or nutmeg.

››››› Wild Rice Soup ‹‹‹‹‹

Serves 4 to 6

With a couple cups of cooked wild rice and some staples usually found in camp, this simple but elegant soup takes only about 15 minutes to make, start to finish.

1 medium onion, minced
6 tablespoons butter or margarine
1/2 cup all-purpose flour or Bisquick
One 10.75-ounce can chicken broth
2 cups cooked wild rice
1/2 cup grated carrots
3/4 cup chopped cured ham
1 cup milk (or cream, if you've got it)
1 to 2 tablespoons dry sherry (optional)
Salt and pepper for serving

In a saucepan, sauté the onion in butter until translucent. Stir in the flour, blending well. Add the broth and bring to a boil, stirring constantly. Boil for a minute or two. Toss in the wild rice, carrots, and ham. Stir, reduce the heat, and simmer 5 minutes or so. Add the milk and sherry, if using. Stir and simmer until nice and hot.

Ladle the rich, thick soup into bowls and serve at once. Let each camper salt and pepper his or her portion to taste.

Chapter 11

Getting Stewed

Quintessential Camp Comfort Food

"Mulligan is the camper's name for the big stew of the evening
meal...the longer it cooks, the better it gets."

—*FIELD & STREAM* EDITOR WARREN MILLER, 1918

HEN IT comes to camp foods, most people
quite naturally gravitate to those that can be
conveniently (usually mercilessly) fried,
grilled, or boiled. While these are certainly among the fastest
methods to cook a hot meal in the woods, they are—counterintuitively—by no means the easiest to master. In fact,
they're among the most unforgiving. There is no correcting
burned bacon, desiccated fish, or overcooked beans. Sadly, the
stew pot is generally ignored. It is thought, quite wrongly, to
take too much time and attention.

Nothing could be further from the truth. For the better
part of four centuries, the stew pot—not the skillet—was the
fundamental piece of cookware in camp. Native Americans,

voyageurs, frontiersmen, homesteaders, cowboys, lumberjacks, and watermen understood its advantages implicitly. Food slowly stewed in a pot retained far more of its flavor, calories (energy), and nutritive benefit (vitamins and minerals) than food fried in a skillet or roasted on a spit. Indeed, in survival situations, even today, experts advise that stewing is the best cooking method for ensuring food safety as well as capturing its maximum value (the energy- and vitamin-rich broth should be relished, not discarded). What's more, as the old-timers knew full well, making a pot of stew involves a minimum of preparation, tending, and fuel, and consequently, is a lot less work for the cook. Beyond keeping up a bed of coals for a few hours, which a well-laid fire generally does by itself, about all the cook really has to do is stir occasionally.

Nothing Is Simpler

If you can simmer water, you can make a good camp stew. With a modicum of imagination, you can easily make an excellent one. The double-barreled appeal of camp stew is its utter simplicity, yet endless variety.

There's absolutely no mystery about it. I once asked an old outfitter's cook the secret. He looked at me like I was a lunatic and growled: "Fill a damn pot with what you got, simmer it two hours, and leave it the hell alone."

He was dead right, of course. The slow burn does all the real work: rendering tough meat tender, dried beans plump, and root vegetables buttery. It works some culinary magic too. The slow percolation of flavors and aromas transforms even the plainest camp fare into extraordinarily tasty comfort food.

This remarkable transformation was perhaps best described by a clerk with the Northwest Company, voyaging west by canoe to his fur-trading outpost in the Canadian bush, in 1780. "The camp kettle was hung over the coals, nearly full of water," he wrote. "Then nine quarts of dried peas—one quart per man—were put in. When they were well bursted [sic], two or three pounds of salt pork, cut into strips for seasoning, were added and then four hard biscuits [hardtack] broken up and stirred into the mess." It seemed impossible that such a dish could be good. But when called to supper, he saw that "the swelling of the peas and biscuit had filled the kettle to the brim—so thick a stick would stand upright in it—and it looked inviting." He "begged the cook for a plate full of it," found it delicious, and admitted, "I happily ate little else during the whole journey."

In fact, such simply made, satisfying camp stews are legendary. In the Northeast, made with any combination of meat and vegetables on hand, they were known as hotchpotch or slumgullion or, more commonly, mulligan. In the South, a stew made with fowl and rice was called purloo or bog. Made with squirrel meat and corn, it was called Brunswick stew. Out west, cowboys appropriately christened jerked beef stewed in flour gravy "jowler"; when bull testicles and organ meats were substituted for jerked beef, they called it district attorney stew. On the water, fishermen called various combinations of stewed fish, shellfish, and vegetables salmagundi or, more universally, chowder. Salt beef stewed with onions and ship's biscuit was lobscouse. Despite the differences in nomenclature and ingredients, the basic cooking method—slow simmering—was identical.

Ironically, the slow cooking that makes stews so good—one to two hours, generally—is exactly why most campers today avoid them. In our fast-food culture, the mere thought of waiting a couple of hours for supper to cook—especially outdoors where everyone's ravenous—is anathema. Eating quickly, not well, is the order of the day. Yet if there is one place where eating well is more welcome and time—gratefully—can still be found and savored, it is in camp.

SATISFYING STEWS

Nobody really has to wait on a stew. Not even the cook. Once the prep work's out of the way (in most cases, 10 to 15 minutes) and the ingredients set to simmering, a stew can pretty much be forgotten. While it's simmering—essentially cooking itself—everyone can do what he or she came to do in the first place. Take your choice: cast or troll for fish, hike, botanize, birdwatch, snooze, read, update a journal, play poker, study maps or the sunset, up-end a dram or two, or just talk, easily and comfortably, about things—memories, plans, and dreams—you don't often talk about at home. Then celebrate by coming together over a singularly distinctive, slow-cooked meal you never have time for back in civilization.

Here is a sampling of time-honored, easily made camp stews. None of them is fancy: in fact, practicality is their greatest virtue. All feature staples universally found in camp or in your local supermarket. With few exceptions, the fresh foods indicated will keep quite well in camps without any refrigeration. The exceptions (mostly fresh meats), if packed in a well-insulated cooler with block ice (never cubes, mind you), will travel well and keep fine for three to five days. When backpacking or canoeing, where ice and coolers are precluded, fresh meats can be hard frozen in freezer bags beforehand and safely carried for a day or two. Beyond that, cured meats (salted, smoked, dried) or vacuum-packed meats can be substituted.

›››››› Nantahala ⟫Jerky⟪ Stew ‹‹‹‹‹

Serves 4

Nantahala stew is an old-time backpacker's favorite: plain, simple, and gluttonously glorious. There are dozens of variations. This one's named for the Nantahala Wilderness, in the western North Carolina mountain range of the same name. Its principal ingredients are marinated dried beef and fresh potatoes, some dried vegetable soup, freeze-dried corn, and instant brown gravy. In camp, its preparation is exceptionally easy.

The only thing you have to do beforehand is make a mess of beef jerky. If pressed for time, you can substitute the store-bought variety, but it's exponentially more expensive and not a fraction as good.

It doesn't take much time or trouble to make the real stuff. And everybody—believe me—will thank you. When suppertime comes, put your fine jerky and the following ingredients to work.

2 large potatoes (14 ounces), diced
One 1.5 ounce packet dried vegetable soup mix
One 1.5-ounce packet freeze-dried corn
One 1-ounce packet brown gravy mix
1 pound beef jerky (recipe follows)

In a large pot, bring 2 quarts of water to a boil, add the potatoes, and cook for about 10 minutes.

Add the soup and corn, and stir. Add the gravy mix and stir again. Simmer for 5 minutes.

Shred the jerky, toss it into the pot, stir, and continue to simmer. It will plump up like fresh beef, redolent of Worcestershire and wine, and fill the pot.

Let the whole agglomeration simmer another 5 to 10 minutes. Not that you really need to time it with a watch: the stew's ready when it's rich and thick enough for a spoon to stand in. Serve hot with toasted English muffins, which keep better than loaf bread, to sop up the gravy.

QUICK-AND-GOOD HOMEMADE BEEF JERKY

1½ to 2 pounds flank steak or London broil

MARINADE:
4 to 5 garlic cloves, chopped very fine
½ cup Worcestershire sauce
1 cup dry red wine

Put the meat in the freezer for half an hour to 1 hour, or until stiff and firm, not frozen. The partial freeze makes it much easier to handle and slice. Remove the meat from the freezer and cut, across the grain, into ¼-inch-thick slices.

In a large bowl, mix the marinade ingredients. Add the meat, cover, and marinate in the refrigerator for 3 hours.

Remove the meat from the marinade and lay flat on a baking sheet. Place in the oven at its lowest temperature setting (usually 140°F), with the door propped open (so air circulates), and leave to dry slowly overnight (8 to 10 hours). Go to sleep. Don't worry about it. In the morning, test a slice: bent in half, it should break. If it doesn't, let it dry another hour or two, until it does. Wrap in aluminum foil and it's good to go—and keep—for days. Eaten as is, it's a wonderful trail snack. In soups or stew, it's sublime.

,,,,, Three More Simple Jerky Recipes <<<<<

Campers who make their own jerky quickly get hooked on the simplicity, economy, and taste of it. Using different meats (beef, fish, poultry) and seasonings, the varieties are virtually endless. The method of preparation—marinate and slow bake—remains the same.

GOURMET BEEF JERKY

The beef here is prepared exactly as it is in the preceding version. The spices and seasonings, however, give it a completely different flavor.

2 pounds flank steak or London broil

MARINADE:
1 teaspoon salt
3 garlic cloves, chopped very fine
1 teaspoon pepper
$1/4$ cup brown sugar
$1/2$ cup teriyaki sauce
$1/2$ cup soy sauce

Partially freeze the meat and cut into $1/4$-inch slices, as directed in the preceding recipe.

In a large bowl, mix the marinade ingredients. Add the meat, cover, and marinate in the refrigerator overnight. Remove the meat from the marinade, lay flat on a baking sheet, and dry in a 140°F oven for 8 to 10 hours or until the meat is brittle.

FISH JERKY

Plain, sun-dried fish is a staple ingredient in dozens of traditional American camp dishes. Using an oven and a modicum of modern ingredients, it can be made quicker and better than ever before. Dried fish is best broken up and simmered in soups or chowders.

MARINADE
1 cup orange or pineapple juice
2 teaspoons lemon juice
2 teaspoons soy sauce
2 garlic cloves, minced

1 pound fish fillets (lake trout, walleye, pike)

In a bowl, mix the marinade ingredients. Add the fillets, cover, and marinate in the refrigerator for 3 hours. Remove the fillets from the marinade, lay flat on a baking sheet, and dry in a 140°F oven for 4 to 6 hours, or until the fillets are brittle and flaky.

TURKEY JERKY

This is easily made from cooked turkey (breasts, legs, or thighs) found in most supermarkets. It makes a spicy centerpiece in trail soups and stews.

MARINADE
$1/2$ cup teriyaki sauce
$1/2$ cup soy sauce
1 teaspoon pepper
Pinch of cayenne

2 pounds cooked turkey, cut into $1/4$-inch slices

In bowl, mix the marinade ingredients. Add the turkey, cover, and marinate in the refrigerator overnight. Remove the turkey from the marinade, lay flat on a baking sheet, and dry in a 140°F oven for 8 hours, or until the meat is brittle.

›››› Hapless Hunter Stew ‹‹‹‹

Serves 4

Some of the best outdoor cooking advice I ever got came from a hunter who had spent almost threescore years in pursuit of game. He delivered it, unsolicited, smoking a briarwood pipe over a steaming kettle of a uniformly brown, but wonderful-smelling substance. "Never forget," he said, "hunting isn't eating." After a nip or two of rum, he revealed the recipe for what he called "hapless hunter stew."

Obviously, you don't need fresh venison or game to make this dish. Cured ham, smoked bacon, Canadian bacon, smoked or dried sausage—all of which travel well in the wild in their preserved state—will serve admirably. This stew's other distinction is that its primary seasoning is brown sugar, not salt. The sweetness, mild but wonderfully flavorful, allows its other plain-Jane ingredients to shine brightly. Preparation is simplicity itself.

2 cups dried beans (any kind you like, I usually use Great
   Northerns)
2 to 3 garlic cloves, minced
2 large potatoes, chopped
1 large onion, chopped
4 celery ribs, chopped
2 cups chopped cured meat (country-cured ham is best, in
   my opinion)
1 cup rice (not precooked or instant)

1 cup corn (fresh, freeze-dried, or canned)
1/2 cup brown sugar
Pepper (optional)

Soak the dried beans overnight. If you find that too bothersome, there's an effective short cut: just parboil them. Place the beans in a large pot, cover them with water, bring to a rolling boil for 2 minutes, and then let stand for an hour or so.

When you're ready to cook—and I use the word loosely—drain the beans, put them in a stew pot, cover with 6 to 8 cups of fresh water, bring to a boil, and simmer for an hour. Go do something more interesting. The beans will be just fine.

When you get back, the only work you have to do is chop up the vegetables and meat and add them to the pot. At the same time, toss in the rice and corn. Actually, at this point, feel free to add practically any other ingredients (fresh, dried, or canned) you like. As with jazz, improvisation only improves a stew.

Cover and simmer another hour. Longer is fine: you can't really overcook it. Occasionally, toss in a palmful of brown sugar, stir, and taste. Toss in more brown sugar if you like. Other than that, leave it alone, unless you feel the need to shake in some freshly ground black pepper. Resist all temptation to add salt. If needed, add more liquid during cooking.

Whenever you want, ladle into big bowls. Serve steaming hot, with crusty bread or biscuits to sop up the gravylike broth.

>>>>> Modernized Brunswick Stew <<<<<

Serves 4

Originally, this was a staple, backwoods camp dish for the poor on the early American frontier. Its principal ingredients were squirrel meat—the most easily hunted and abundant game to be had (a square mile of good woodland can hold over 600 squirrels)—stewed with the only crops that could be grown in the pioneers' small forest clearings: corn, potatoes, and beans (actually black-eyed peas, called cow peas, since they were principally used to feed livestock).

Since then, it's been gastronomically glorified with the addition of ingredients generally unavailable to eighteenth-century Appalachian homesteaders. Among these are tomatoes, which the pioneers thought were poisonous; onions, which they didn't cultivate (relying on wild ramps, or scallions, instead); and chicken, which they kept exclusively for eggs and reluctantly slaughtered only when they'd stopped laying. Consequently, today's myriad recipes for Brunswick stew are profoundly different from one another and their various merits hotly argued.

Fortunately for today's camp cook, yesterday's basic recipe still works. With a singular exception. Since few of us nowadays have the skill for "barking" squirrels—shooting a rifle or musketball into a tree trunk close enough to the animal for the concussion or fragmented tree bark to bring it down in more or less one piece—store-bought chicken must substitute. An economical three-pound stewing hen, either frozen or fresh and stowed in an ice chest, will do. Back of beyond, where this is an encumbrance or impossibility, one to two pounds of retort-packaged chicken will do equally well. You'll usually find retort-packaged meats shelved with canned meats in supermarkets. Nutritionally, the two are nearly identical. But the retort packages, essentially flexible cans, are lighter, easier to pack (in and out), require no can opener, and make less garbage—good things for campers.

Stewing up this approximation of the original recipe is equally easy and just as good. It's a dish best made in a cabin, hunting shack, or fish camp with a propane or conventional range.

1 stewing chicken (approximately 3 pounds) or
    equivalent of retort-packaged chicken
1 large red onion, diced
2 cups corn (fresh, freeze-dried, or canned)
5 medium potatoes, sliced thin
6 tomatoes, chopped (fresh or canned)
1 cup black-eyed peas (fresh or canned)
Salt and pepper

In a large pot, boil the chicken in water to cover until the meat falls off the bone, about 1 hour. There's nothing else for the cook to do until it does. When done, separate the meat, discard the bones, return the meat to the chicken stock. If using vacuum-packaged chicken, add to canned chicken stock.

Add the vegetables and stir. Add chicken meat. Liberally salt and pepper, cover, and let the stew simmer for 1 hour or until thick.

Serve with skillet-made cornbread (page 105) or—better yet—dumplings cooked in the stew (page 156).

›››› Crowded Chowder ‹‹‹‹

Serves 4

Chowder is no more than a waterman's stew. Legions of them are memorable. This one, however—first enjoyed at a broken-down duck-hunting shack in the salt marshes of Barnegat Bay in

1972—comes always and particularly to mind. Because the engine of the friend's boat taking us there conked out twice on the way, we arrived with wrench-skinned knuckles at dusk in a cold downpour and grim mood, unsure we'd be able to get back to the mainland.

Providentially, a woman in the party had brought a pot of "crowded chowder"—so named because it's shoulder-to-shoulder with minced clams, bay scallops, and lump crabmeat. Simmered on a single-burner propane range, it reversed our fortunes. The warped, marine plywood shack admitted every chill, salty night breeze, but we slept wondrously well fed and warm.

Any waterman or water fowler should learn this recipe by heart.

1 bunch scallions, chopped
4 celery ribs, chopped
2 medium potatoes, chopped
3 cups milk
8 ounces minced clams (fresh or canned, as your circumstances warrant)
8 ounces bay scallops (ditto)
8 ounces lump crabmeat (ditto)
Salt and pepper
Butter

In a large pot, bring 1 quart salted water to a boil. Add the scallions, celery, and potatoes, return to a boil, reduce the heat, and cook 5 to 6 minutes or until tender. Add the milk, stir, and simmer for about 5 minutes or until steaming hot, but not boiling. Add the clams, scallops, crabmeat, and their liquor. Allow these to just heat through, about 5 minutes. Season to taste with salt and pepper.

Ladle into bowls, top each with a pat of butter (it's rich enough without it, but richer still with), and serve.

>>>>> Unlucky Angler Chowder <<<<<

Serves 2

There is no way to make a disappointing catch go farther—or taste better—than when stewed into a hot, bracing chowder. I first witnessed this improbable trick performed almost 20 years ago. Near the end of a Canadian canoe trek, my partner and I were stormbound on a small island in the middle of a vast, angry lake, our provisions just about exhausted. A solemn day's shore fishing in pouring rain yielded one small northern pike, or jackfish as it's called in Canada, where it's routinely discounted as a junkfish, too bony to eat. We would have released it, but for the fact it had irretrievably swallowed a lure. It could not have weighed more than a pound and a half whole—not enough to make a decent meal, much less a memorable one.

My fellow paddler, however, lit a cigar—his last—and showed me otherwise. Under a tight-pitched rain tarp, he assured me that the foul weather would soon pass and there would be plenty of big fish ahead. From the water-logged food pack, he pulled out our remaining provisions: dry milk, dried soup, margarine, a couple of sprouting potatoes, half an onion, and some sour-smelling slices of bacon. In the rain, he proceeded to whip up a remarkable meal. The measures of ingredients are approximate, but as near as I can recollect.

2 medium potatoes
1/2 yellow onion
4 slices (4 ounces) bacon
1/2 cup dry milk
One 1.5-ounce packet dried vegetable soup mix
3/4 to 1 pound fish fillets, cubed
Bisquick or all-purpose flour
Margarine

Bring a pot of water to a boil (about 4 cups). Dice potatoes, onion, and bacon (the finer, the better) and toss them into the pot. Simmer about half an hour.

Add the dry milk and soup mix. Stir well.

Add the fish. Let simmer 5 to 6 minutes, no longer.

Remove the pot from the heat, stir in a palmful of Bisquick to thicken the broth, dab with margarine, and dig in.

⟩⟩⟩⟩⟩ Carolina Bog ⟨⟨⟨⟨⟨

Serves 4 to 6

This rich, peppery camp stew originated in the early 1800s in the Carolina lowlands, where rice, waterfowl, and game birds like wild turkey, bobwhite quail, woodcock, and mourning doves were plentiful. Today, as in Brunswick stew, chicken has taken the place of game. Otherwise, its traditional ingredients remain unchanged and distinctively American: from red and green bell peppers and tomatoes (native to the Americas) to country-cured ham and sausage. Some say it's called bog because that's where the birds originally used to make it came from; others because, simmered brown, it looks like tannin-stained bog water. Whichever: all agree it's a comfort-food feast in a pot.

Like most traditional camp stews, there are hundreds of different variations of "original" bog. I've chosen one of the simplest. It's best made in a cabin or outpost camp where you've got a steady-burning propane range to cook with.

2 tablespoons bacon fat or vegetable oil
2 green bell peppers, chopped fine
2 red bell peppers, chopped fine
4 white onions, chopped fine

4 celery ribs, chopped fine

4 garlic cloves, minced

2 pounds fresh tomatoes, chopped (or two 15³/4-ounce
    cans chopped tomatoes)

2 cups dry red wine

4 tablespoons (¹/2 stick) butter (for roux)

¹/4 cup flour (for roux)

1 pound cured ham or country sausage, coarsely chopped

Two 10¹/2-ounce cans chicken stock

1 pound boneless chicken thighs (about 4)

Salt

Black pepper

Red pepper or Tabasco

Cooked white rice

Melt the bacon fat in a large stew pot. Add the peppers, onions, celery, and garlic and cook over medium-high heat until soft (10 minutes or so). Add the tomatoes and wine; stir. Bring the mixture to a boil, reduce the heat, and simmer for 10 to 15 minutes.

While the stew is simmering, whip up a roux. Some camp cooks find this intimidating; it's not. Melt the butter in a small skillet, add the flour, and stir until smooth. Cook over medium heat, stirring, until the roux is brown as bog water (about 10 minutes); add to the stew and stir.

Add the meat and chicken stock to the stew, stir well, and let simmer over low heat for 40 minutes or more.

Chop up the chicken thighs and toss them into the stew pot. Season with salt, black pepper, and ¹/2 teaspoon of red pepper and stir. Let simmer for 20 minutes or more—the longer, the better. Bog will happily simmer for hours and only get more flavorful.

Ladle over steaming white rice and serve.

»»»» Field-made Cassoulet ««««

Serves 4

I know it's lunacy to think anything as substantial and time-consuming as a good cassoulet can be made creditably in the woods. In a backpacker's bivouac, no less—with no more than a stew pot, skillet, and good bed of coals.

An old friend and camping companion of mine, Jim Badonsky (an artist, designer, and camp cook), first showed me how this was done in the last place I ever expected: smack in the middle of Georgia's 45,000-acre Cohutta Wilderness, the largest wilderness area in the East. We had backpacked all day and forded the swift-running Jacks River four times before we made camp. I was expecting a supper of macaroni and cheese. Instead, as the last of the sun caught the spruce trees above Horseshoe Bend, Jim produced something quite wonderful. For a first- or second-night backpacking dinner, it is hard to improve upon.

To forestall the legions of ascetic backpackers who'll carp and claim this dish is too damned perishable and heavy to carry into the wild, I'll respectfully disagree—having gladly, and without mishap, carried my share of it into various extremely rugged wilderness areas. As stipulated, it's intended to make a first or second night's supper. Under most conditions, the meats, if hard frozen, will keep that long.

On longer backpacking trips, you can substitute retort-packaged turkey (usually found with canned meats in supermarkets) for fresh chicken thighs and dried beans for canned and make a reasonable facsimile of this dish. According to Jim, however, "It has to be real andouille and fresh thyme or it's not worth the trouble."

2 tablespoons olive oil
1/4 cup flour

4 bone-in chicken thighs
2 andouille sausages (about 1 pound), cut in 1-inch pieces
1 carrot, sliced
1 onion, chopped
1 celery rib, chopped
3 garlic cloves, chopped fine
1/4 cup red wine
12 sprigs fresh thyme
Pepper
Two 12-ounce cans cannellini beans (or 1 pound dried
    beans, cooked, see page 184)

Heat the olive oil in a stew pot. Place the flour on a plate, dredge the chicken in the flour, and place in the pot and brown on all sides. Remove and set aside.

Add the sausage, carrot, onion, celery, and garlic to the pot and sauté until the sausage is lightly browned and the onion is translucent (10 to 12 minutes). Add the wine, thyme, pepper, and beans, and stir thoroughly.

Lay the chicken atop the mixture and press down until almost covered. Cover the pot and set on low coals. Cook, checking occasionally (savoring the rich aroma), for about an hour. Serve at once.

PART VI

➡️

Vegetables

CHAPTER 12

YOU DON'T KNOW BEANS

Beans are the main standby, portable, wholesome, and capable of going far, besides being easily cooked, although curiously enough a great deal of mystery is supposed to lie about the bean-pot.

—JOHN MUIR, 1869

WHEN DANIEL Boone set out on his "long hunts" into the wilderness, he took his rifle, knife, hatchet, a copy of *Gulliver's Travels,* and a pack mule loaded with—among other necessities—dried beans, salt pork, and molasses. With these ingredients, he could cook up what generations of hunters and anglers have hankered for ever since: pork and beans, Boston baked beans, bean soup, or a dozen other delectable dishes.

Few camp foods go farther (a pound of dried beans, about 2 cups, makes 12 servings), last longer (they'll keep for up to a year), or contain more nourishment than the humble dried bean. And no food makes a better one-pot camp meal.

The only trade-off beans require is cooking time. Which is usually why most outdoorspeople today leave them behind. Dried beans should be soaked overnight before cooking. But dropping a few cups of beans into a pail of water before turning in is no great amount of labor (no more than dousing the campfire). And if that's too much trouble, there's a very effective short cut: parboiling. Just cover the beans with water (an inch or two deep), bring them to a rolling boil for about 2 minutes, and let them stand an hour or so while you go do something more intriguing. Like take a nap. The bean is patient. It will wait for you. And as in many other things in life, and particularly in the field, patience brings the greatest rewards.

More to Beans

★

Native Americans called beans one of the "Three Sisters"—beans, corn, and squash. In addition to the preceding camp dishes, you can use beans to make a mouthwatering succotash (see page 205). You can just as easily make a classic Cajun dish using red beans and rice and a dash of Tabasco. Or black beans and rice with shredded onion. Or pinto beans and rice with green and red peppers.

One thing's certain. The more you know about beans, the more you'll want to take them on your next trip in the field.

Now, you could pack along canned pork and beans in tomato sauce, or what are labeled "baked beans," but they're faint imitations of the real thing. They are side dishes, at best, mere reheated substitutes, not beans as they were originally meant to be—a slow-cooked, satisfying main course for ravenous outdoorsmen. It's precisely the time element that makes dried beans so good. Beans absorb the essence of whatever they're cooked with (pork, onion, and molasses), yet still impart their own unique flavor. And that flavor varies from bean to bean.

The Canadian voyageurs carried dried pea beans (the smallest of the white beans) and salt pork and happily ate little else, canoeing all the way from Montreal to Grand Portage at the head of Lake Superior and back. Long hunters like Boone packed along the beans that grew best in their small fields—usually black-eyed peas, also called cow peas, since they were principally used to feed livestock. Cooked with some fatback, however, they made a rib-sticking meal. Western trappers, overlanders, and cowboys relied on pinto beans (pink and speckled like trout), which took longer to cook than other dried beans, but were worth it when cooked with smoked bacon.

Although cooking beans takes some time, they require remarkably little trouble. Fortunately, at a deer shack (when the day's hunt is over) or fish camp (when the fish refuse to rise), there's an abundance of time. That's the perfect time to lay up one of America's quintessential campfire meals. If you're in camp with a propane range or oven, it's practically effortless. But any of the following recipes can just as easily be made in a Dutch oven covered with coals, a collapsible reflector oven set in front of the fire, or a kettle hung or set on a grill over coals. Try any one of these dishes and you'll never go back to canned beans again.

››››› Hunter's Bean Pot ‹‹‹‹‹

(from George W. Sears's classic Woodcraft and Camping, 1884)

Serves 4 to 6

This is the original pork and beans: a plain, hearty, time-honored nineteenth-century camp dish. It takes time (three hours) and it's definitely plain. Our forefathers had plenty of the former and as for the latter, they were principally hungry, not picky. You might want to liven it up with onions, chiles, or hot sauce. It's a dish best reserved for layover or fixed camps, where time and fuel aren't concerns.

2 cups dried beans
1 pound salt pork
4 large potatoes, sliced thin
Salt and pepper
Tabasco

Parboil the beans as described on page 184, remove from heat, and let stand for an hour or so. Put the salt pork in another pot—don't slice, chop, or dice it; leave it in one big chunk—and add water to cover. Bring to a boil and simmer for 30 minutes.

Drain the pork and the beans; place both in a pot with 3 cups water. Bring to a boil and let simmer for 1½ to 2 hours. Go smoke your pipe, consult your tackle box, or invite your Muse.

When the time's up, add the potatoes, pressing them down among the beans until fully covered. Add salt to taste, a liberal amount of pepper, and simmer another 30 minutes. Remove from heat, ladle the beans and potatoes into bowls (or tin plates, whichever you have) and thinly slice the pork on top. Dash with hot sauce and—as Muir wrote— "Announce supper by the call, 'Grub!' "

>>>>> Camp Baked Beans <<<<<

Serves 6

Baked beans, of course, are a different animal entirely from boiled pork and beans. Real baked beans, made the old-fashioned way, require a helluva lot more time—up to 8 hours—but little more attention. In a cabin or camp, however, the smell of this slow-baking dish will whet appetites all day and greatly enhance your reputation as cook. Furthermore, there will likely be enough left over to eat cold the next day (on bread, slathered with some hot mustard, baked beans make excellent sandwiches). Navy beans, so-called because they were a staple aboard ships for 500 years, are best here. Given the baking time involved, it pays to double this recipe and make a big batch all at once. Stowed in a camp cooler or fridge, the beans will make a satisfying side dish (hot or cold) for days.

2 cups dried white beans
$^{1}/_{2}$ pound salt pork, diced
1 large onion, chopped
$^{1}/_{2}$ cup molasses or maple syrup
1/2 cup honey or $^{1}/_{4}$ cup brown sugar
2 teaspoons dry mustard
Salt and pepper

Fill a large pot or Dutch oven with water and soak the beans overnight. In the morning, drain the beans, rinse, cover with fresh water, bring to a boil, and simmer 30 minutes.

Remove the beans from heat and drain. In the same pot, add the remaining ingredients, enough water to cover, and stir well.

Put the pot, covered, into the camp's oven preheated to 250°F and go away for 6 to 8 hours while it slow-bakes. Whoever is left in camp should be charged to check it occasionally to see if the water has baked away. If it has, just add more, stir, and let simmer.

Before serving, remove the lid and bake a few more minutes to allow the beans to brown on top. Then dig into some deliciously sweet, aromatic, and tender baked beans—as they were intended to be eaten.

››››› Stewed Black-eyed Beans ‹‹‹‹‹

Serves 4

Daniel Boone likely ate something very much like this, because it's quick to make, involves ingredients that keep without refrigeration, and will amply feed a hungry crew. It can all be done in a big skillet. This bean stew makes an excellent breakfast, lunch, or dinner. The black-eyed peas—combined with the bacon— made a complete carbohydrate-, protein-, and fat-balanced meal. Boone and his hunters took to the woods well fed.

1 cup dried black-eyed peas (soaked overnight or par-
    boiled; see page 184)
1 pound smoked slab bacon, chopped
1 medium onion or bunch of scallions, diced
2 large potatoes, chopped
1/4 cup molasses
Pepper

Boone would have soaked the peas overnight. In the morning, he would have sliced eight to ten rashers of bacon off the smoke-cured slab in his saddlebag, chopped it up fine, and fried it over the coals in a skillet. When it was almost done, he would have added the peas, onion, and potatoes, stirred it all together, poured in 1 or 2 cups of water, and left the concoction to boil on the coals for half an hour. After that time, he'd top it with a liberal drizzling of blackstrap molasses, a fistful of pepper, wait another quarter hour, and then call the boys to the fire.

EATING WITH DANIEL BOONE

★

One of America's most enduring outdoors images is of a lone, buckskin-clad frontiersman vanishing for months in the wilderness, roaming free and living entirely off the land. Armed with only a long rifle, hatchet, and knife, powder horn and shot pouch over one shoulder, a half-blanket and haversack of parched corn over the other, he not only braved the wild, he conquered it.

The image, however, is dead wrong.

So-called long hunters—the first whites to venture over the Appalachian Mountains to hunt and trap in the game-rich grounds of modern-day Kentucky and Tennessee—did not travel alone, light, or casually. Indeed, they planned their hunts as carefully as modern mountaineers plan Himalayan ascents—especially the food.

For his first long hunt into the Kentucky wilderness in 1769, Daniel Boone left nothing to chance. Though no one rejoiced in wilderness more, it was strictly a business proposition for him: a yearlong trip over the mountains to bring back deer hides and fur pelts to sell. Living entirely off the land was not his plan: it would take far too much time away from the important business of hide hunting and trapping. So Boone loaded his pack mules with 50-pound sacks of stone-ground white cornmeal and parched yellow corn (kernels baked in hot ashes until brown). In smaller sacks were dried green beans (sun-dried to an appearance and consistency called "leather britches") and dried peas (black-eyed peas). In yet smaller sacks were dried apples, dried pumpkins (cut into rings and sun-dried), and cellared sweet potatoes. Sewn tight in cheesecloth (to keep out flies), were whole, dry-cured hams and sides of dark-smoked back bacon. He took corn whiskey and sorghum syrup in watertight, five-gallon kegs. In twists six feet long, he took cured Virginia tobacco to chew during the day and smoke in pipes at night.

Boone's canny choice of these provisions was based on wilderness experience. Though he knew nothing about the modern-day calorie count (energy content) of foods, he knew that cornmeal fueled hungry men better than flour (indeed, it contains more calories than either wheat or rye). It was also cheaper and kept better. He knew that dried peas were winter feed for farm animals, but were somehow sustaining enough by themselves to keep oxen fit all winter and would feed hunters just as well. The dry-cured hams and bacon he took along were lighter, more compact, and more impervious to spoilage than their equivalent of salt pork or beef in wooden casks pickled in brine.

Pound for pound, the cellared sweet potatoes he brought were better suited to wilderness appetites than potatoes (they contain one-third more calories and are naturally sweet). His homemade sorghum syrup (pressed from an Indian corn–like plant) was cheaper and contained one-fifth more calories (an amazing 14,080 calories per gallon) than imported dark molasses, which backwoodsmen like Boone couldn't afford in the first place. The parched corn he packed could be munched dry as a trail snack, rehydrated to plumpness in soups or stews, or fed to pack animals to supplement meager forage. Likewise, the dried apples and dried pumpkin, which kept well, were equally tasty, and welcome either boiled or eaten dry. If food ran short, the calming, appetite-suppressing properties of his home-grown tobacco (nicotine)—along with his 100-proof corn liquor (10,660 fire-breathing calories per gallon)—would happily supply the shortage.

Camp gear was selected for maximum utility and durability, much of it state-of-the-art stuff for the time. For cooking, Boone took nesting brass or copper kettles, which were lightweight and compact—precursors of today's backpacking mess kits. Indeed, such nesting kettles were among the most popular trade items on the frontier. Heavier cast-iron Dutch ovens and "spiders" (four-legged skillets designed to sit above a bed of coals) were taken for baking and frying. For sleeping, he took "three-point" trade blankets (each "point" roughly designating one pound of good English wool) instead of deer or bearskins. They were not only lighter, but insulated even when wet, dried faster, and could be washed.

For the same reasons, most frontiersmen like Boone didn't wear buckskin clothing except for moccasins and leggings, if they could help it. They preferred homespun garments of "linsey-woolsey," which was a sort of 60/40 fabric of its day: a sturdy, coarse weave of linen (noted for its strength) and wool (renowned for its warmth). In fact, the thing most emblematic of the legendary frontier rifleman was the ubiquitous, linsey-woolsey "hunting shirt." This tough, lightweight smock reached to the knees. It was purposely cut loose for freedom of movement and versatility. Wrapped around and belted at the waist (no buttons or hooks to lose), it made a very effective carryall. The belt secured a hatchet, knife, and pouch containing flint, firesteel, and tinder. Above the belt, the billowing shirt served as a haversack that could easily accommodate quarts of parched corn or the meat of any game taken along the way. It was caped at the shoulders and fringed along its hems and sleeves—not for decoration, but to shed rain. It was dyed with the hulls of shelled nuts (acorn, butternut, and walnut)— not for color, but camouflage.

Rousted from his blankets in the predawn Kentucky darkness, a long hunter found the camp keeper had breakfast well underway. Sizzling in a skillet were thick slices of smoked bacon. Steaming in a kettle was cornmeal mush drizzled with sweet sorghum. Baking in a Dutch oven, its top bright with coals, was fragrant, hot Indian bread. As the hunter wolfed this down, accompanied by a dram or two of corn whiskey, the camp keeper wrapped the leftovers in a kerchief for lunch. The cold Indian bread (called corn dodgers) could be eaten as is. The cold mush, cut into squares, could be fried with bacon fat at midday. If the hunter was to be gone a day or more, the camp keeper doled out sufficient cornmeal, side bacon, and parched corn to feed him until his return.

CHAPTER 13

SQUASH

The Most Misunderstood Camp Vegetable

We laid waste acres of Indian Cucumbers [zucchini], Squashes
[winter squash], Simblems [summer squash] and Pompions
[Pumpkins] of such size as cannot be equaled at home.

—MAJOR GENERAL JOHN SULLIVAN, 1779

QUASH, AN original staple, indeed indispensable,
Native American camp food, was revered by the
Indians—with corn and beans—as one of the
"Three Sisters." As much as its siblings, it sustained American
Indian nations from the arid Southwest, throughout the river
bottoms of the Southeast, to the forests of the Midwest and
Northeast. Rich in energy (carbohydrates), packed with nutrients (20 percent or more of an adult's recommended daily
value of vitamin C, vitamin A, potassium, and magnesium),
easily stored whole or dried, and deliciously prepared in a
hundred various ways, it sustained the first European
colonists and generations thereafter, too.

Like so many other native foods they hungrily expropriated, however, the Europeans just couldn't get their tongues around its proper name. In Algonquian, the vegetable was called *isquotersquash* or *askutasquash* which, roughly translated, meant "a green thing eaten raw."

Europeans at the time seldom ate anything green or uncooked. Neither actually did the natives, who first cultivated squash about 5,000 years ago. To the contrary, native cooks roasted or baked squash whole or chopped their firm, sweet meat into chunks to sauté in bear oil or stew with venison or fish. Alternatively, once cooked, the fleshy meat could be mashed or whipped into a fine consistency to make savory puddings or velvety soups. No part was wasted. The seeds, slow-roasted to bring out their nutty flavor, made an excellent snack. The squash blossoms, picked just before they opened, were either plunged into boiling water (for about a minute) and served as a side dish, or dipped in cornmeal batter and fried in oil to make succulent appetizers. However prepared, the vegetable, in its myriad forms—acorns, butternuts, crooked and straight necks, pattypans, turbans, and massive Hubbards—made delightfully good eating. The Europeans—more anxious to eat it than categorize its bewildering varieties—dismissively called them all squash.

The importance of this all-American crop, to Indians and colonists alike, was starkly apparent. During the American Revolution, Major General John Sullivan led a punitive expedition of 4,000 Continental soldiers into the heart of the pro-British, Iroquois Confederacy in upstate New York. Its principal objective wasn't to destroy the warriors of the Confederacy (who numbered no more than 1,000), but the foodstuffs upon which they and their families depended for the upcoming winter. In the late summer of 1779—harvest time—he burned more than 40 Iroquois villages to the ground, chopped down every tree in their orchards, and torched more than 160,000 bushels (4,500 tons) of dried corn and beans. He paid particular attention to obliterating all the squash he could find, destroying 3 million pounds (1,500 tons) of the "handsomest" he'd ever seen. Considering the Iroquois at the time numbered but 10,000 in all (men, women, and children), that amounted to roughly 300 pounds of squash per capita—a measure of its vital place in the food chain. The loss of this food broke the power of the Iroquois forever.

Nowadays, however, squash is something of the Rodney Dangerfield of vegetables. Most Americans use them for decoration. Pumpkins are carved into Halloween jack-o'-lanterns, of course. The colorful, dried gourds of other varieties are arranged in holiday centerpieces (along with dried Indian corn). If squash is eaten at all, it's generally once or twice a year (invariably on Thanksgiving or Christmas), as a side dish or in pies, or occasionally soup, and it generally comes from a can or the frozen foods section.

Ironically, you almost never see this traditional American camp food in camp. It's universally thought to take too much time and trouble to bother with. In fact, it takes no more than a bed of coals, a kettle of boiling water, or a hot oven.

⟩⟩⟩⟩⟩ Spit-roasted Acorn Squash ⟨⟨⟨⟨⟨

Serves 4

Squash (potatoes and onions, too, for that matter) are particularly good spit-roasted over wood coals or charcoal. So-called winter squashes—thick-skinned varieties like acorn, butternut, and spaghetti—not only keep well in camps without refrigeration, but also are rather self-contained cooking vessels in themselves. All you need to spit-roast fresh squash are a couple of deadwood sticks, a coat hanger (10-gauge wire) from home, and a glowing bed of coals.

2 acorn squash
4 tablespoons ($^1/_2$ stick) butter or margarine
Cinnamon
Salt and pepper

Stake two forked sticks (to support the spit) on opposite sides of a lively bed of coals swept from the campfire. Naturally forked sticks—to support the spit—will be found in the woodpile from which you made your fire. If not, notch with a knife. Spit squash on coat hanger and position them about 6 inches above coals. Roast, turning the spit occasionally (wear a heavy glove or oven mitt; the wire can get damned hot), for 45 to 50 minutes, or until the squash are easily pierced by a knife.

Remove the squash from the spit, split into steaming halves, and scoop out the seeds. Dab with butter and sprinkle with cinnamon, salt, and pepper.

>>>>> Baked Summer Squash <<<<<

Serves 8

This is definitely best made in a summer cabin or cottage, where fresh produce and refrigeration are available. It's so rich and sweet that it is more of a pudding than a side dish, but that's what makes it so memorable.

10 summer squash, sliced
2 medium onions, chopped
6 large eggs

1 cup milk
8 tablespoons (1 stick) butter
Pepper

Preheat the oven to 250°F. In a pot, boil the squash and onions in water to cover until tender. Drain. Add the remaining ingredients and mix well. Place in a baking pan and cover. Bake for 25 to 30 minutes, or until puffy. Uncover pan at end to brown on top.

>>>>> Sautéed Skillet Squash <<<<<

Serves 4

Softer-skinned summer squash—crookneck, white or yellow scallop, or green zucchini—are ideal for cooking in a cast-iron skillet. Combined with a few camp staples, like onions and cheese, they quickly make a substantial, distinctively tasty side dish.

2 tablespoons oil, butter, or bacon grease
1 large onion, chopped
4 small summer squash (any variety), cubed
One 4-ounce can chopped green chiles
2/3 cup grated Cheddar cheese

In a skillet, heat the oil. Add the onion and sauté until tender. Add the squash and sauté, stirring, for about 5 minutes or until tender. Add the chiles, stir well, and simmer 2 to 3 minutes more. Add the cheese and stir until melted. Serve immediately.

>>>>> Grilled Squash <<<<<

Serves 4

This recipe comes straight from the U.S. Forest Service, which has been feeding rangers, fire lookouts, and fire-fighting crews for over a century. If its hard-boiled, voraciously hungry veterans endorse a dish, that's ample recommendation for the rest of us. The sole adaptation made here is the substitution of real garlic for the horrid garlic powder used in the original.

1 medium zucchini
2 small yellow (summer) squash
Salt and pepper
4 garlic cloves, minced
4 tablespoons ($^{1}\!/_{2}$ stick) butter or olive oil

Slice the squash in long spears. Place on a sheet of aluminum foil big enough to completely wrap around the squash. Sprinkle the salt, pepper, and garlic over the spears. Top with butter and seal in foil. Place the foil package on a grill over hot coals for 10 to 15 minutes, or until the squash is tender. Remove from the grill and eat out of the foil.

»»»» Squash Fritters «««

(adapted from Buster and June Ducan)

Serves 6

Fried squash fritters, served alongside fresh-caught fish, make a wonderful summer camp feast. They're quite as easy to make as the usual fish fry side dishes (potatoes, hush puppies, etc.), but twice as good because they are not expected fare.

2 cups grated summer squash
1/2 cup all-purpose flour
2 tablespoons grated onion
2 tablespoons brown sugar
1 tablespoon salt
2 large eggs, beaten
2 tablespoons butter, melted
2 to 3 tablespoons vegetable oil

In a bowl, combine all ingredients except the vegetable oil and mix well. Heat the oil in a skillet. Drop spoonfuls of the mixture into the skillet and fry like pancakes. Add more oil as necessary.

★ CHAPTER 14 ★

CORNUCOPIA
All-American Camp Food

Corn has a distinctive flavor unlike that of any other grain.

—FOOD AUTHORITY HAROLD MCGEE

F ALL America's native foods, maize—which the Europeans called "Indian corn"; in fact they called all grains, whether wheat, rye, oats, or barley, "corn"—was perhaps the single most important. It is even more so today. After wheat and rice, it is now the third largest human food crop in the world. Considering corn was completely unknown outside the Americas until a mere 500 years ago, that's nothing short of astonishing.

Ironically, it was apparently the last of the sacred "Three Sisters" (squash, beans, and corn) to be domesticated by Native Americans. The large-grained wild grass—teosinte (*Zea mexicana*)—was first cultivated in central Mexico between 4,500 and 3,500 B.C., roughly 1,000 years after squash and beans. It wasn't widely grown, however, until sometime after 200 A.D. Yet by the time of European contact, it had become the chief dietary staple of the Americas. Indeed, among its most advanced cultures—the Maya, Inca, and Aztec empires—it was a deity. A cruelly demanding one, requiring unremitting human sacrifice.

Though the Europeans didn't deify corn, they very quickly came to depend upon it quite as much as the Indians. It was the salvation of colonists from Jamestown to Plymouth and Santa Fe to Savannah. Indeed, historian Arthur Parker wrote that corn "was the bridge over which European civilization crept, tremblingly and uncertainly, at first, then boldly and surely to a foothold and a permanent occupation of America."

Nowadays, though you might not recognize it, corn—in one form or another—is far more than a bridge. It's intrinsic to the foundation of day-to-day life. The beef, pork, and chicken you eat are all corn fed. Corn syrup sweetens your favorite soft drinks, ice cream, and just about every other processed sweet food or beverage you buy. Cornstarch thickens your canned, baked, and frozen foods. Corn oil not only makes your margarine, it's used to fry your potato chips, pretzels, and cheese puffs—virtually any snack foods you eat. Corn mash is at the heart of most of your favorite beers and liquors (particularly bourbon whiskey). Corn and its by-products are also used in manufacturing, packing materials, and plastics.

The one place corn is usually missing—fresh, succulent sweet corn, that is—is in camp. In many ways, that's understandable. It's bulky to pack and, being largely water, quite heavy: about three average-size ears to the pound. An ear doesn't go far: cut from the cob, it will yield only about half a cup of kernels. And compared to other fresh fruits, grains, and vegetables, it doesn't keep well at all: two to three days, at best, before its sugar turns to starch and the corn turns flavorless. Consequently, on all but short camping trips, where you can justify the weight and plan to eat it the first or second night out, fresh corn is better left at home.

On backpacking and canoe trips, where the weight of fresh or canned corn precludes carrying either, freeze-dried corn is an admirable substitute. In fact, of all freeze-dried fare, I would judge whole-kernel corn the best. A standard-sized packet weighs just $1^1/2$ ounces and rehydrated will make one cup (two servings) of corn that's virtually indistinguishable from fresh. The downside, as in all freeze-dried foods, is its expense: $3 or more per $1^1/2$-ounce pouch. At home, this seems excessive. In the bush—where the sweet, crunchy, fresh-tasting kernels make a stand-alone side dish or enliven stews, soups, and chowders—it will seem a bargain.

If you can't pack fresh, canned, or freeze-dried corn, you can still—with minimal weight, expense, and effort—enjoy it the old-fashioned way: dried or ground into meal.

On most camping trips, however, of whatever duration, you'll be well advised to take some fresh corn to delight in for a day or two. You will be long remembered for it.

»»»» Roasted Ears ««««

Serves 4

Fresh-picked corn on the cob, properly prepared, is one of the finest of all traditional American camp foods. Among the simplest and most effortless to make, it is also—sadly—the most commonly ruined, typically because campers today don't make it the traditional Indian way. Most shuck the ears and either boil them in a pot of scalding, salted water or wrap them in aluminum foil and steam them on a bed of hot coals.

They're far better (and easier) roasted Indian style.

8 ears fresh corn, unhusked
Melted butter
Salt

First and foremost: leave the husks intact. The corn silk, too. It's Mother Nature's packaging and a near-perfect cooking container.

Light a wood or charcoal fire and let it burn down to a bed of red-hot coals. Lay the unhusked ears on a grill over the coals (you want to roast it, not steam it). Some like to soak the ears in water beforehand, but I don't find it improves them. Cook for 7 to 10 minutes, turning a few times, until the husks just blacken at their edges. Remove from the grill, strip off the husks and silk (they'll peel away easily when hot), dip in melted butter, and sprinkle liberally with salt.

>>>>> Skillet-fried Corn <<<<<

Serves 4

This dish was a great favorite on the frontier. It is just as popular today in camps where fresh corn is at hand. The salty smoked bacon and tangy onion complements the sweetness and crispness of the browned (caramelized) corn. For lunch, serve alongside BLT sandwiches. For dinner, garnish the corn with crumbled bacon and serve as side dish.

8 ears fresh corn
$^{1}/_{4}$ pound smoked bacon
1 large onion, chopped
Salt and pepper

Cut the corn kernels from the cobs into a bowl; you should get about 4 cups. As a general measure, an ear of fresh corn will yield from $^{1}/_{2}$ to $^{3}/_{4}$ cup of kernels. With the back of a knife, scrape the pulp and juice from the cobs into the same bowl. The pulp and succulent juice make the dish. Set aside.

In an iron skillet, over a bed of lively coals (medium-high heat, if you're cooking on a stove), fry the bacon and set aside. Drain about half the hot bacon grease from the skillet. Add the onion and sauté until translucent. Add the corn kernels, pulp, and juice to the skillet and fry, stirring regularly, until the kernels are nicely browned (6 to 8 minutes). Season with salt and pepper to taste, and serve.

⟩⟩⟩⟩⟩ Succotash ⟨⟨⟨⟨⟨

Serves 4

The Pilgrims took a great liking to Algonquian-made *msick-quatash*, a hearty mixture of boiled corn and beans. The dish, stewed with bear fat or acorn oil, was unlike anything they'd tasted in the Old World. Made of two foods altogether unknown to them—"indian corne" and lima beans—it tasted singularly and freshly of the New.

Few people make succotash the old-fashioned way anymore. It's quintessentially celebratory, summer harvest fare, best made with fresh-picked beans and new corn cut from the cob. In back-packing and canoe camps, of course, this is generally an impossibility (though freeze-dried corn and beans can make a facsimile). In drive-in or fly-in camps or cottages, however, where the fresh ingredients can be easily transported, it's a midsummer dream.

2 cups fresh lima beans
1/2 cup salt pork, diced
1 medium onion, chopped
1 garlic clove, minced
2 cups fresh corn (about 4 ears)
4 tablespoons (1/2 stick) butter
3/4 cup milk or 1/2 cup heavy cream
Salt and pepper
Tabasco (or other hot sauce)

Put the beans, salt pork, onion, and garlic in a saucepan with enough water to cover by 2 inches. Bring to a boil, then reduce the heat and cook 5 minutes, no more. Remove the pan from heat, drain, and set aside.

In an iron skillet over medium heat, sauté the corn kernels

in butter for 3 to 5 minutes, stirring constantly. Add the bean mixture and stir well. Pour in the milk and just enough water to cover. Simmer 15 minutes or until the liquid is reduced, stirring regularly.

Remove from heat, stir well, and add salt and pepper to taste. Add a dash or two (or three) of Tabasco and dish out.

››››› Baked Cracker Corn ‹‹‹‹‹

Serves 6

Virtually all pioneer homesteads had four things in common. They grew corn, had at least one milk cow, kept some egg-laying hens, and had access to a trading post or country store, which— if it had nothing else—had a barrel filled with unleavened, hard-baked crackers variously called hardtack, ship's bread, or Boston crackers. These crackers were cheap and kept virtually forever. Eaten by themselves, they were godawful. Cooked in combination with the pioneers' homegrown fare, however, they made a wonderful camp dish.

2 tablespoons butter
1/4 cup chopped onion
1/2 green pepper, chopped
2 cups fresh corn (about 4 ears)
2 cups milk
2 large eggs, beaten
12 saltines or similar crackers, pounded fine

Preheat the oven to 350°F. Butter a baking tin. In an iron skillet, heat the butter over medium heat. Add the onion and pepper and sauté for about 10 minutes or until the onion is translucent. Add the corn, milk, eggs, and saltines and pour into the baking tin. Place the tin inside a large pan and pour in enough water to come halfway up the sides of the baking tin. Bake for 45 minutes. When a knife inserted in the center comes out clean, it's done.

»»»»» Savory Corn Cakes «««««

Serves 4

Don't let the longish list of ingredients keep you from trying these traditional, delectable cakes. The recipe has only three fresh vegetables, after all, combined with staples found in virtually any fixed camp or cabin. Just chop and sauté the veggies, mix them with the batter, and fry.

2 to 3 tablespoons vegetable oil
3 bell peppers (green, red, yellow, or a mix), chopped
1½ cups fresh corn (about 3 ears)
3 bunches scallions, chopped
½ cup cornmeal
2 tablespoons all-purpose flour
½ teaspoon baking powder
1 teaspoon salt
2 large eggs, beaten
½ cup milk

Heat the oil in a skillet and add the peppers, corn, and scallions. Cook for about 5 minutes and set aside.

In a bowl, combine the cornmeal, flour, baking powder, and salt. Add the eggs and milk and mix well. Add the sautéed vegetables and mix again. You will have a thick, lumpy batter. If the mixture is too dry, add water by driblets until it is evenly moist.

Heat a well-greased skillet. Drop the mix by big spoonfuls into the pan, and fry about 2 minutes on each side or until the cakes are a rich, golden brown. Serve immediately.

⟩⟩⟩⟩⟩ Cornmeal Blueberry Biscuits ⟨⟨⟨⟨⟨

Makes 8 to 10 biscuits

The joy of making these is picking the blueberries yourself. However, a sensible degree of caution is necessary. Blueberries are a favorite food of black bears. From late summer until the first frost, to put on weight for their winter hibernation, they'll strip every bush they can find. So before approaching a blueberry patch, make as much noise as you can: shout, blow a whistle, bang on pots, sing, yodel. The bears will give you a wide berth.

1 cup self-rising white or yellow cornmeal
2 tablespoons margarine
1/2 cup milk
1 teaspoon sugar
1/2 cup fresh blueberries

Let the campfire burn down to hot coals. If in a cabin or camp with a conventional oven, preheat to 450°F.

Grease a large sheet of aluminum foil.

Put the cornmeal in a bowl and cut in the margarine. Add the milk, sugar, and berries and stir until just blended. Drop spoonfuls of batter onto the foil and place in a reflector oven before a bed of bright-burning coals. Bake for 15 minutes or until a wood splinter inserted in a biscuit comes out clean. If using a conventional oven, bake for 12 to 15 minutes.

★ CHAPTER 15 ★

TATERS

Campers' Favorite Vegetable

Almost anyone can cook potatoes, but few cook them well.

NESSMUK (GEORGE W. SEARS), 1920

➤★

IRONICALLY, OF the legions of unknown, exotic vegetables encountered by the Europeans in the Americas—which included artichokes, beans, bell peppers, chiles, pumpkins, squash, and tomatoes—the most humble now reigns supreme. The native Inca called it *pappatata*, which the Spanish conquistadors mispronounced *batata*, and the English-speaking world later corrupted into *potato*.

Though cultivated and prized as food by the Indians of South America for 2,000 years before the arrival of Europeans (at the time of contact, the Inca had domesticated over 400 species), the Spaniards thought the lumpish, many-eyed tuber fit only for animal fodder. In 1580, they shipped but one species home *(Solanum tuberosum)*—for use as ornamental foliage in formal gardens. Hardy, easily grown, and tolerant of a wide range of conditions, however, the plant quickly proved suitable, not only for ornamenting gardens, but also for cheaply feeding peasants as well as animals. Within the comparatively short span of two centuries, the potato spread across Europe, from Russia to Ireland. Today it's the most widely grown vegetable on earth and—after wheat, rice, and corn—the most important food crop on the planet.

It's not surprising America's ugly duckling veggie is so popular. A medium potato weighs only about five ounces, yet contains 100 calories of quick energy, half a day's value of vitamin C, a quarter of the DV of potassium, plenty of fiber, plus substantial amounts of vitamin B-6, niacin, riboflavin, and thiamin. It also packs beneficial amounts of essential minerals like iron, magnesium, phosphorus, and zinc. Contrary to popular opinion, it's not loaded with carbohydrates: indeed, a medium potato contains only 9 percent of an adult's total daily allowance. If you were solely dependent on potatoes for carbs, you'd have to eat 11 of them a day to meet your daily requirement. Self-contained and long keeping in its tough skin, the potato is arguably among Nature's most nutritious, efficient food packages.

Certainly, it's America's favorite vegetable. Per capita, Americans eat about 130 pounds of potatoes a year—equivalent to about one medium potato every day. Sadly, more than half the potatoes Americans eat aren't fresh, but factory-processed in one way or another (canned, frozen, dehydrated, freeze-dried). In camp—for all the wrong reasons—the percentage is probably much higher.

I remember an argument at a fly-in fishing camp with a buddy who had—unilaterally—decided to ditch fresh potatoes in favor of canned and instant ones. This crushed all hope of making spit-roasted potatoes, potatoes baked in their jackets, firm-boiled potatoes, crisp-fried potatoes, shredded potato pancakes, and crunchy hash browns. It reduced us to reheating precooked, canned spuds or—worse—a boiled water porridge of powdered potatoes.

He held up his canned and packaged potatoes in defense and said, "These will keep for years." I told him that was no culinary endorsement and, since our stay was to last two weeks, irrelevant. "These are already peeled and cooked," he said. That, I told him, was precisely why they were no damned good. The skins of potatoes are where most of their nutrients and flavor lie. Stripped of these and precooked, little good or flavorful is left: nothing worth looking forward to, at any rate. "These are easier to pack and carry," he said. I told him that a pound of fresh potatoes weighed no more than a pound of canned ones (less, considering the weight of the can), and that instant potatoes—however compact, easy, and prolific—could never be made whole or wholesome again. A week of eating processed potatoes converted him. Halfway through our trip, when the outfitter flight-checked our camp, he ordered a five-pound sack of Idahos.

››››› Sand-baked Potatoes ‹‹‹‹‹

Serves 4

Many well-meaning camp cooks unwittingly ruin baked potatoes. Almost invariably, they mummify them in aluminum foil and either bury them in the coals of a wood fire or stick them in an oven. In the coals, they burn into bricks. In the oven, they don't really bake, but are steamed into a starchy mush.

This dirt simple (pardon the pun) method, on the other hand, makes near-perfect soft, white, flaky baked potatoes. The hunter who showed me how to do it couldn't recall who'd showed him and didn't think it much of a secret. Thick-skinned Idaho or russets, the all-purpose baking potato, are fine; personally, though, I find thinner-skinned white potatoes better.

4 medium to large potatoes, scrubbed
Sand (foraged from riverbank, lakeside, or seashore)

Preheat the oven to 400°F.

Fill a 4-quart kettle about three-quarters full of sand and bury the potatoes in it. Place the kettle (uncovered) in the oven and bake for about 1 hour, or until the potatoes are easily pierced with a fork. Remove the potatoes (using tongs, knife, what have you) and rinse with hot water (from the pot a wise camp cook always has on hand for brewing after-dinner coffee or tea and washing dishes). Serve piping hot.

››››› Camp-made Potato Pancakes ‹‹‹‹‹

Serves 4

Ordinarily, nobody bothers to make real potato pancakes in camp anymore. Most cooks think you have to peel and boil the potatoes first (you don't) or that grating them's an onerous chore (it isn't). In fact, preparing the whole business takes about 15 minutes.

Cooking them is effortless (who can't flip pancakes?). Eating them—fried golden, wonderfully textured, tangy with onion— is pure pleasure. With eggs and ham, they're wonderful for breakfast. With fried fish, they're ideal for supper. Single servings of applesauce (light and requiring no refrigeration) make a great accompaniment.

4 medium potatoes, scrubbed and unpeeled

1 medium onion

2 large eggs, beaten

½ cup bread crumbs (cracker or potato chip crumbs work equally well)

1 tablespoon salt (omit if you use potato chips)

1 teaspoon pepper

2 to 3 tablespoons butter, margarine, or oil)

Coarsely grate the potatoes into a bowl (if you don't have a grater in camp, you can improvise one by punching holes in an empty can). In the same bowl, coarsely grate the onion. Add the eggs, bread crumbs, salt, and pepper, and mix well.

Melt the butter in a skillet. Plop large spoonfuls of the mix into the skillet and flatten with a spatula into ¼-inch-thick pancakes. Fry until nicely brown on one side. Turn and brown the other side. Serve immediately.

>>>>> Pencil Fried Potatoes <<<<<

Serves 4

Only tenderfeet peel and boil potatoes before making French fries out of them (or anything else, for that matter). It's a waste of time, effort, and fuel in camp, not to mention taste, texture, and nutrition. The secret is to cut them into thin strips just before consigning them to the boiling oil. They'll emerge crisp on the outside, firm yet tender on the inside, and quite heavenly over all.

2 cups vegetable oil

4 medium to large potatoes, scrubbed and unpeeled

Salt (kosher is best because it clings to the fries better)

In a skillet, heat the oil until it's bubbling hot (about 375°F). As it heats, slice the potatoes thinly, cut into thin strips (about 1/4 inch wide, or roughly the width of a bootlace).

Drop handfuls of strips into the oil and fry for 5 to 7 minutes or until nicely golden. Drain on paper towels (newspaper or brown paper bags will do just as well) and sprinkle liberally with salt. Serve immediately or keep in a 250°F oven until needed.

››››› Camp Boiled Potatoes ‹‹‹‹‹

Serves 4 to 6

If there's a better way than this to make delicious boiled potatoes, I've yet to find it. Small ($1^1/2$- to 2-inch diameter), new (or more accurately, immature) potatoes work best. It doesn't matter whether they're red or white; there's absolutely no difference in taste between the two.

If you want to try an old woodsman's variation, add 1 cup of cracker crumbs (pounded coarse) to the buttered potatoes. Cover the pot and shake-rattle-and-roll it until the potatoes are white and floury with crumbs. Don't use store-bought bread crumbs for this: they'll melt into gum on the potatoes. Only roughly smashed table crackers (saltines, Ritz, whatever) will work.

12 to 16 new potatoes (2 to $2^1/2$ pounds), scrubbed
6 to 8 tablespoons butter
Salt and pepper to taste
Parsley, fresh chopped or dried

Fill a pot with enough water to cover the potatoes, bring to a screeching boil, add the potatoes, and continue boiling over medium heat for 10 to 15 minutes or until just tender. Pour off the water and return the pot with the potatoes to low heat, shaking occasionally, until the potatoes are dry to the touch. Add butter, salt, pepper, and parsley, and stir until the potatoes are well coated with butter. Serve immediately.

»»»» Camp Hash Browns ««««

Serves 4

Any time you're frying bacon for breakfast is the perfect time for frying up a batch of genuine hash browns, too. In doing so, the camp cook can kill two birds with one stone.

3/4 pound bacon
3 garlic cloves, minced
3 small onions, diced
3 medium potatoes, diced
Salt and pepper
Tabasco or other hot sauce
    (optional)

In an iron skillet, fry the breakfast bacon until crisp. Drain on paper towels (or a paper bag), then crumble about one third of the strips ($^1/_4$ pound) and set aside for the hash browns. Pour off about half the bacon fat, add the garlic and onions, and sauté over medium heat until the onions are translucent, not brown.

Add the potatoes, stir in salt and pepper to taste, cover the skillet, and cook 5 to 7 minutes, or until the potatoes are tender. Remove the cover, sprinkle the crumbled bacon on top, and press the mixture flat (don't stir).

Turn the mixture when it's browned on the bottom. The cake may come apart in the process, but no matter: just turn the various parts until well browned. Drain (on paper towels, newspaper, or brown bags). Serve hot and let everyone dash with Tabasco as desired.

★ CHAPTER 16 ★

CABBAGES AND KINGS

A Keeper for Campers

Cabbages put into a hole in the ground will keep well during the winter, and be hard, fresh, and sweet in the spring.

—*THE AMERICAN FRUGAL HOUSEWIFE*, 1829

AMONG **ALL** the longer-lasting fresh vegetables you can pack into the wild—potatoes, carrots, onions, parsnips, turnips, squash—only one of them is green, the common green cabbage. Yet few people today invite it home, much less along on a camping trip. It's generally considered a dinner companion to poverty: cheap and filling, but vile smelling, mushy, and tasteless. Indeed, prepared in the usual manner—boiled to oblivion along with an equally unfortunate chunk of corned beef—it is.

So why on earth haul a head of cabbage, which typically weighs a pound or more (80 to 90 percent of it water), to camp to make what nobody really likes at home anyway?

First: nothing else green keeps longer (three to four

weeks) or goes further (one head will produce about eight cups of shredded cabbage) in the bush without refrigeration. Nor is anything else green more impervious to mishap. I once watched a head of cabbage bounce like a soccer ball down a steep, rocky portage trail, plummet over a fuming waterfall at its foot, and vanish into a bouldered minefield of whitewater beyond. A mile downriver, we found it waiting for us in an eddy: bobbing happily and undamaged but for a bruise or two.

Second: anything fresh, green, and crisp is especially welcome in the backcountry where ironically—unless you're an accomplished wild plant forager, favored by season, weather, and time—it's nearly impossible to come by.

Third: it's probably the most versatile, easily prepared green vegetable you can hump back of beyond. It's excellent raw in quick salads and slaws, briefly boiled or braised as side dishes, or simmered with ham or sausage as a main course. In fact, it's excellent prepared virtually every way except the way everybody in camp expects: the dreaded overcooked, smelly, colorless corned beef and cabbage that Mom used to make. If you're a good camp cook, you'll steer clear of that. With the following simple recipes you can make common cabbage into a king.

>>>>> Classic Camp Cabbage <<<<<

Serves 4

Overboiling cabbage is murder in the first degree. To make it into one of the finest vegetable side dishes you'll ever taste in camp (I promise), try "flash boiling" it instead. It will be crisp, buttery, tart, green cabbage of a sort few of your companions have ever savored.

1 small green cabbage, quartered
4 tablespoons (¹/₂ stick) butter or margarine
Salt and pepper
Juice of ¹/₂ lemon
2 teaspoons dried tarragon

Bring a large pot of salted water to a furious boil. Drop the cabbage into the pot and "flash boil" for about 2 minutes— until it's scarcely tender, yet still wonderfully crunchy and flavorful.

Drain immediately. Season each quarter with a tablespoon of butter (more if you like), a healthy shake of salt and pepper, a squirt of fresh lemon, and a sprinkling of tarragon and serve.

››››› Braised Cabbage ‹‹‹‹‹

Serves 4

"Flash boiled" cabbage (see the preceding recipe) may change some minds about this vegetable. But better yet, forget boiling cabbage altogether. Braised and browned in bacon fat, it's a green dish of distinction in the woods.

4 garlic cloves, minced
6 slices smoked bacon, chopped
1 small green cabbage, shredded
¹/₄ to ¹/₂ cup white wine, beer, or water
Pepper
2 tablespoons soy sauce (optional)

In a deep skillet, fry the garlic and bacon until well browned. Add the cabbage, stir to coat with bacon fat, and braise until the cabbage wilts and is lightly browned. Add wine, cover, and simmer for 5 to 8 minutes or until the wine has evaporated.

Remove from heat; sprinkle on pepper, dash with soy sauce if desired, and serve. Delectable.

»»» Campers' Cole Slaws «««

As a side dish to fried fish, potatoes, or hush puppies, a crunchy, freshly made cole slaw is the near-perfect salad of the woods. There are thousands of variations. Here are four in which the mix of fresh raw vegetables and the accompanying dressings change subtly, but quite distinctly.

CABBAGE AND CARROT SLAW

Serves 4 to 6

This variation is best made in camps where a refrigerator or ice chest is available (for keeping mayonnaise and chilling the salad).

$1/2$ small white cabbage, shredded
$1/4$ small red cabbage, shredded
2 carrots, shredded

DRESSING:
$1/2$ cup mayonnaise
2 tablespoons cider vinegar
1 tablespoon milk (optional)
$1/2$ tablespoon sugar

In a large bowl, mix the cabbages and carrots. In a separate small bowl, whisk the dressing ingredients, pour over the vegetables, and toss until thoroughly coated. If you can, chill before serving. If not, serve as soon as mixed.

CABBAGE-PEPPER-ONION SLAW

Serves 4

1 small green cabbage, shredded
1 green pepper, chopped
1 small onion, chopped

DRESSING:

3 tablespoons vinegar
2 tablespoons vegetable oil
2 tablespoons sugar
1 teaspoon salt

Prepare as in Cabbage and Carrot Slaw (see preceding recipe).

CABBAGE-CELERY-RELISH SLAW

Serves 4

This is another variation best made in camps where a refrigerator or ice chest is available for keeping the mayonnaise.

1 small green cabbage, shredded
4 celery ribs, chopped

DRESSING

6 tablespoons mayonnaise
3 tablespoons pickle relish

1 hard-boiled egg, chopped
1 tablespoon vinegar
1 teaspoon salt

Prepare as in Cabbage and Carrot Slaw (see page 220).

››››› Backpacker's Bare-bones Slaw ‹‹‹‹‹

Serves 2

On a three- to four-day backpacking trip, hauling everything on "shank's mare" (afoot), there's no real excuse for denying your party a fresh-made slaw. Indeed, whipping one up will impress them no end. Just hold off making it until the third or fourth day, when the last fresh vegetables and dried fruits are sure to be appreciated.

$\frac{1}{4}$ green cabbage, shredded
$\frac{1}{2}$ carrot, shredded
1 teaspoon salt
2 tablespoons raisins

DRESSING:
Juice of $\frac{1}{4}$ lemon
2 tablespoons sugar
2 tablespoons milk
Crushed nuts (whatever you've got)

Mix the cabbage and carrot in a bowl and sprinkle with salt. Add the raisins and mix again. In a separate small bowl, mix the lemon, sugar, and milk thoroughly, pour over the vegetables, and stir until well coated. Garnish with crushed nuts and serve.

CHAPTER 17

WILD THING

America's Rice

I dispatched two canoes to fetch the 49 bags
of Oats [wild rice] traded for.

—FUR TRADER JOHN SAYER, 1804

VETERAN NORTHWEST Company trader John Sayer, wintering on the Snake River in central Minnesota more than 200 years ago, obviously held wild rice in high regard. Otherwise he would not have sent two "north canoes," each 25 feet long and capable of carrying 1½ tons of cargo, along with eight of his ten voyageurs, to fetch it. Estimating conservatively, they returned with some 4,000 pounds.

That, of course, was far more than Sayer and his men could conceivably eat in the seven-month trading season (October to April). Indeed, to do so would have required each of them to consume over 1½ pounds of wild rice every day, a rather staggering 20 servings apiece. But feeding his men was not

Sayer's purpose. He was, instead, shrewdly buying up the fall harvest to deny it to competing fur traders and sell it back to hungry natives in the depths of winter—when a sack of wild rice traded for five prime beaver pelts.

The delicious, exceptionally long-grained, wild grass (it's not really rice)—which grows only in North America's upper Great Lakes region—was well worth the price. From Superior to Saskatchewan, it was among the most coveted of all native foods. It was energy rich: a pound contained 1,800 calories. It was also nutritious, with significant amounts of vitamins A, B-2, B-6, calcium, niacin, phosphorus, potassium, and zinc. Most important, parched (slow-roasted) and stored in a cool, dry place, it kept well for years: insurance against starvation.

Even better, for the Native American nations fortunate to live where it thrived, wild rice was perennial, a sure crop that only had to be harvested. Unlike corn, beans, and squash, cultivated south of the Great Lakes, it required no hard labor (girdling trees, breaking ground, planting, hoeing weeds, scaring off crows and deer) nor did it deplete the soil after a few seasons. Harvesting it was as simple as paddling into a rice stand, bending the grass stalks over a canoe, and gently beating the grain-heavy heads with sticks until the canoe was filled with them. Furthermore, since kernels of wild rice on the same stalk ripen at different times, the same rice beds could be harvested two or three times every season. This made natives of the rice-growing lands far less dependent on seasonal farming and nomadic hunting and fishing than their neighbors.

In a land of feast or famine, such a perennially growing, high-energy, simply harvested crop was a very rich annuity. Not surprisingly, it attracted murderously jealous eyes. In fact, for the better part of three centuries, the native nations around the Great Lakes battled for control of the wild rice beds quite as fiercely as Europeans of the same period warred for cultivated farmland.

By comparison, the seemingly high price of wild rice to-day—about $2 for a six-ounce box of the cultivated variety, more for the same amount of the genuine, wild-grown arti-cle—isn't excessive. In fact, considering that a six-ounce packet of freeze-dried wild rice and mushrooms costs about $6, the raw rice is a bargain. Since both raw and freeze-dried wild rice contain about the same number of calories and the nutritional content of the former is vastly superior, it's a steal.

Yet you seldom find it in any camp. From backpackers' bivouacs to fancy weekend rental cabins, America's native, cool-climate wild rice (Zizania palustris) has been almost uni-versally abandoned in favor of nonnative, industrially culti-vated, tropical white rice (Oryza). Economies of scale being what they are, it's far cheaper than wild rice: indeed, white rice yields about 4,000 pounds per acre, while wild rice yields only about 200 pounds per acre. But its main attrac-tion is that it cooks up to five times faster. Cheap and fast, however, are hardly gustatory or nutritional recommenda-tions. Convenience, as always, has its price. Instant rice—which is precooked (parboiled) and stripped of its original nutrients and then, ironically, "enriched" or "fortified" with synthetic ones—has fewer calories, half the fiber, and fewer vitamins and minerals than an equal amount of unprocessed, slow-cooking wild rice. What's more (or rather less), one pound of instant rice will make about eight servings, while a pound of wild rice will make 20 to 25.

So far as taste and texture are concerned, there is no com-parison. The difference between the two is as vast as that be-tween instant and whole-bean coffee (see Chapter 6). Indeed, wild rice is much like whole-bean coffee, in a way. In large measure, its natural flavor and aroma (and nutrients) are captured when its whole grains (kernels) are slow-roasted. When boiled, those kernels "flower" (burst) into a crisp-textured, nutty-flavored, fragrant dish that naturally complements fresh-caught fish, venison, and fowl, smoked bacon, jerked beef, and dried sausage. There is no finer side or main dish in the forest and lake country of the north.

››››› Simple Wild Rice ‹‹‹‹‹

Serves 4 to 6

Cooking plain wild rice is so easy it hardly merits description. The sole objection to taking it on a camping trip is that cooking it simply takes too much time and fuel. Admittedly, it takes 30 to 45 more minutes to prepare than instant rice, but if you're counting minutes on vacation, you need a vacation from your vacation. And it does take more fuel to cook (30 minutes' "burn" time versus 10). In camps where economizing on cooking time and fuel are paramount (primarily mountaineering and back-packing, where you're moving camp every day and hauling both food and fuel), those are weighty concerns. Quick, fuel-efficient preparation of calories takes precedence over good eating, and raw wild rice (or any other uncooked, whole-grain rice, for that matter) is generally better left behind.

Happily, on the majority of camping trips most of us take, no such sacrifice is necessary. One cup of raw wild rice swells to about four cups when cooked. Whenever making wild rice in camp, it's always a good idea to cook up somewhat more than twice what your party can eat at one sitting. It saves time and fuel the next day and spares the cook any extra work. Cooked rice can be used afterward to make pancakes, fish cakes, soups, stews, and salads quickly and easily.

1 cup (6 ounces) raw wild rice
4 tablespoons (¹/2 stick) butter or margarine
Salt and pepper

In a large pot, bring the rice and 4 cups water to a boil. Reduce the heat, cover, and simmer for 40 to 50 minutes. If you like your rice soft, cook longer. If you like it chewier, cook less. Remove from heat and let stand for 10 to 15 minutes, or until the rice is the desired texture (al dente to tender). Drain. Add butter, season liberally with salt and pepper (since wild rice is sodium-free), mix well, and serve.

›››› Wild Rice, Cranberries, and Nuts ‹‹‹‹

Serves 4 to 6

This is a change-up on the basic wild rice every camp cook should know. It's just as easy to make, but it elevates the already distinctive taste of wild rice to a wilder, crunchier, tarter plane. Just as important, it convinces your camp mates that you're do-ing some impressive culinary gymnastics. In fact, all you're really doing is boiling the rice in broth instead of water, and mixing in ³/4 cup of the unexpected. You will, of course, never reveal this. Like magicians, camp cooks keep their secrets.

1 cup (6 ounces) raw wild rice
One 10¹/2-ounce can chicken broth
¹/4 cup chopped nuts (almonds, crushed walnuts, pecans,
    even canned water chestnuts)
¹/2 cup dried cranberries
Pepper

In a large pot, bring the rice, broth, and $1^1/2$ cups water to a boil. Reduce the heat to low, cover, and simmer 30 minutes. Add the nuts and cranberries, mix well, and simmer 5 minutes. Remove from heat and let stand, covered, 10 to 15 minutes. Drain. Season with pepper to taste (there's really no need to add salt; the broth has plenty) and serve.

››››› Wild Rice Pancakes ‹‹‹‹‹
⟩Breakfast and Supper Versions⟨

While cooked wild rice is the basis for both of these traditional camp favorites, they're, well, wildly different. As different as day and night, in fact: perfect for breakfast or supper. In the morning, mixed with flour, milk (whether fresh, retort-packaged, evaporated, or dried), and eggs (fresh, freeze-dried, or powdered), leftover rice makes superlative hotcakes. At dusk, mixed with chopped onions, eggs, and salt, it makes a wonderfully savory side dish. With leftover wild rice from the night before, any cook can whip these up in 15 minutes or less. Be advised: wild rice pancakes are considerably thicker, denser, more substantial, and filling than all-flour hotcakes. This recipe will make 12 to 14 of them, more than enough to feed four. They're equally good with butter and maple syrup, or spread with jelly, jam, preserves, honey, or peanut butter (you're in camp, so go ahead and play with your food).

BREAKFAST WILD RICE PANCAKES

Serves 4 to 6

2 cups all-purpose flour or Bisquick

1 cup milk

2 large eggs
1 cup cooked wild rice
2 tablespoons butter or margarine, melted

Grease a skillet and heat it until a drop of water sizzles in the pan.

In a bowl, mix the flour, milk, and eggs into a batter, just as if making regular pancakes. Mix in the rice and butter. Pour $\frac{1}{4}$ cup of the mixture per pancake into the hot skillet. When they bubble around the edges, flip and gently brown the other side, then serve immediately.

SUPPER WILD RICE PANCAKES

Serves 4

Serve hot just by themselves as a side dish, well sprinkled with salt. Topped with ketchup, or especially applesauce, they're even better.

3 cups cooked wild rice
$\frac{1}{2}$ cup finely chopped onion
2 large eggs
1 tablespoon salt
1 tablespoon pepper
Ketchup or applesauce, for serving

Grease a skillet and heat it until a drop of water sizzles in the pan. Mix the rice, onion, eggs, salt, and pepper in a bowl. It will make a rather slippery mess that looks nothing like pancake batter, but don't worry about it. Drop handfuls of this amorphous mixture into the hot skillet. Press flat with a spatula (the pancakes will firm as they cook). Fry until golden brown around the edges, turn, cook the other side likewise, and serve with ketchup or applesauce.

»»»» Baked Wild Rice Stew «««««

Serves 4 to 6

It sounds like double-trouble to make, but this traditional North Woods dish really isn't. Using leftover wild rice, it takes only about 15 minutes of prep time and little more than an hour in the oven (either electric, propane, or wood-fired). For a hearty main course, it's hard to beat. The can of condensed cream of mushroom soup may seem at odds with the otherwise fresh ingredients involved; nonetheless, it's traditional, having been a backwoods staple since its introduction by the Campbell Soup Company in 1934.

2 pounds stew meat (or 1 pound bacon)
1 large onion, chopped
1 cup sliced mushrooms (about 15 or 20)
1 cup chopped celery
4 cups cooked wild rice
One 10½-ounce can condensed cream of mushroom soup
Salt and pepper for serving

Generously grease a baking or roasting pan and preheat the oven to 350°F. Grease a large skillet and preheat it until hot.

Brown the meat in the hot skillet (if using bacon, dice it and fry until tender, not crispy) and set aside. In the same skillet, sauté the onion, mushrooms, and celery until the onions are translucent (3 to 4 minutes) and set aside.

In the baking pan, combine the rice, mushroom soup, meat, and vegetables and mix well. Cover with aluminum foil and bake for 1 to 1½ hours. Serve and pass the salt and pepper.

>>>>> Wild Rice Salad <<<<<

Serves 4 to 6

OK, it's not really a salad in the conventional sense of the word. But in camps where conventional salad-making ingredients (fresh tomatoes, spinach, lettuce, and the like) are scarce or nonexistent, and cold storage space (whether propane fridge or ice chest) is at a premium, it makes a damned fine substitute. Remember to keep the mayonnaise cold, in any case.

2 cups cooked wild rice
2 large apples, chopped fine (Granny Smiths are best)
6 tablespoons raisins (or 2 of the ready-to-eat, $1\frac{1}{2}$-ounce boxes you keep for snacks)
Juice of $\frac{1}{2}$ lemon
2 tablespoons sugar (white or brown, or maple syrup)
3/4 cup mayonnaise
1 orange, peeled and sliced thin

In a bowl, mix the rice, apples, raisins, lemon juice, and sugar. Combine with the mayonnaise and immediately put in your camp fridge or ice chest for a couple of hours. Serve cold, topped with orange slices.

PART VII

★ CHAPTER 18 ★

BIG MEDICINE

Strong Drink in the Wild

On the first day of the journey, the cork came out of the whiskey keg and spilled more than half, to Mr. Tootle's great disappointment. Indeed I don't believe he has recovered from it yet.

—MRS. ELLEN TOOTLE, OREGON TRAIL, 1859

I'M SURE Mr. Tootle didn't recover until he'd reached Fort Laramie, nearly halfway to Oregon. The sutler's store there would have been his last chance at whiskey east of the Rockies. This should not (necessarily) be mistaken for intemperance. Emigrants like the Tootles, crossing the continent by wagon train, were explicitly advised by the U.S. Army to "take from 5 to 10 gallons of whiskey to a wagon" plus a bottle of brandy. Officially the whiskey was "to purify bad water" and the brandy "for medicinal purposes." The real reason, as the army well recognized, was to maintain morale on the man-killing, six-month-long, 1,600-mile journey west.

None of this escaped the notice of Mr. Tootle, who apparently understood the importance of whiskey to morale quite as implicitly as the army. He embarked a 10-gallon keg. This wasn't a drop more, he likely told Mrs. Tootle, than the army recommended. As he likely didn't tell her, that amounted to fully 850 jiggers (or 1,275 shot glasses) of potent (90–100 proof) corn whiskey. Enough to boozily carry him—come hell or high water—for six months, at $4^{1}/_{2}$ jiggers (6.75 ounces) per day, across the wilderness into the Promised Land.

Losing more than half of it the first day on the trail was much more than just a libationary disaster for Tootle. It was a financial one as well. On the trail, whiskey, quite literally, was portable wealth in liquid form. Emigrants used it in lieu of cash to pay farriers, ferrymen, and wheelwrights. In trade, it could be bartered more quickly and profitably than anything else in an emigrant's wagon. The farther west one went, the more valuable it became. In St. Louis, a gallon of whiskey cost 20 cents. At Fort Laramie, a gallon fetched $10. How much whiskey Tootle bought at Laramie to refill his stash and, more important, what outrageous price he paid for it and whether or not he ever told Mrs. Tootle about it, are details lost to history.

One historical fact is certain: few camps and cabins on the American frontier were without alcoholic beverages for long, and then only as long as it took to remedy the situation. Anything—gathered or grown—that could be fermented, distilled, and drunk, pretty much was. Whiskey was made from corn, rye, barley, or wheat. Wine was made of everything from native American, Catawba, Concord, and Delaware grapes to chokecherries, blackberries, elderberries, salmonberries, and loganberries, down to dandelions, clover, even rose petals ("One of the finest [wild wines]," according to a pioneer). Vegetables—carrots, potatoes, parsnips, pumpkins, and rhubarb—were also made into wines. Indeed, "Calamity Jane Wine" was made from potatoes, carrots, *and* rhubarb. Although vegetable wine sounds terrible, some are actually quite good; a bottle of Wisconsin-made pumpkin wine, consumed on a Canadian fishing trip, resembled French sauterne.

Brandy was distilled from apples into applejack, from pears into perry, and from peaches into what was called, of course, peachy. Hard ciders, fermented from the same fruits, were generally all called hards. Indeed, most frontier orchards weren't planted to provide fruit, preserves, jams, or pies, but largely for the raw materials to make strong drink. Home-brewed beers were concocted of everything from spruce needles to camas roots to cactus leaves.

Partly, this was sheer practicality. Livestock and humans commonly contaminated streams and wells. On the frontier, cholera, typhoid, and other waterborne diseases killed far more people than anything else did. Pioneers quickly learned that water was best boiled before drinking. For reasons they could not understand, nobody got sick that way. But all that boiling—all the labor of cutting wood, splitting it, and tending the fire—produced only a flat, insipid liquid that quenched thirst but little more. In contrast, that same water and same fire, combined with some homegrown grain, fruit, or vegetable and some ingenuity, could be rendered into firewater.

It's almost universally assumed that Europeans introduced alcohol into the Americas. In fact, the Incas and Aztecs had been making corn beer (*chicha*), cactus whiskey, (*pulque, tequila,* and *mescal*), and other intoxicating beverages for centuries. Drunkenness, however, was rare: by Aztec law, public intoxication was punishable by death. On the other hand, Aztec law allowed the elderly to drink all they wanted, as long as they caused no public disturbance.

No such laws applied to the first Europeans who arrived in ships, which, more often than not, were sunk to their gunnels with hogsheads (140-gallon barrels) of liquor, brandy, wine, and beer. Strong spirits were thought essential to good health. Wine and beer were sensibly shipped in lieu of water, which, after a few weeks at sea in wooden casks, turned green, stinking, and undrinkable with algae. Indeed, the principal reason the notoriously abstemious Pilgrims made landfall at Plymouth Rock was because they ran out of beer. Out of beer, they were quite literally out of water. According to the *Mayflower*'s log: "We could not take time for further search or consideration [of a landing place]; our victuals being much spent—especially beer."

WHAT TO TAKE

The best spirits to take into the wild, as old-timers will attest, are those that stand on their own or require no adulteration but plain water. Rum, whiskey, and brandy fit the bill perfectly.

Though many of my favorite bartenders will no doubt disagree, in order of priority I'll offer a list of libations best suited for the wild.

RUM

For the better part of 300 years, rum was the drink of choice in the North American wilderness, primarily because it was the preferred liquor of the first Europeans to truly penetrate the interior: the French *courers de bois* and voyageurs, the Scotch-English fur traders, the American mountain men. These hardies knew their stuff. On extended trips, to drink themselves and to trade for pelts, they wanted maximum proofage and minimum weight.

They found it in concentrated light Puerto Rican or dark

Jamaican rum. Fermented and distilled from the residue of sugar cane (molasses), it was simply and cheaply made, stunningly potent (up to 151 proof), easy to ship via America's myriad inland waterways, and improved with age. In primordial forested country, where Europeans had yet to clear and cultivate land for other liquor-producing crops (rye, barley, wheat, corn), rum was the all-purpose elixir.

It mixed with cold water to make a simple grog scarcely to be improved upon. Mixed with boiling water and sugar, it made a restorative hot toddy. With boiling water and a few pats of butter, it made a fat-rich, superlatively warming nightcap. Taken straight, it raised hair. It was also good for cooking.

››››› Basic Grog ‹‹‹‹‹

This is the old-fashioned camp standard.

1 teaspoon sugar
Juice of $1/4$ lemon
1 jigger ($1^1/2$ ounces) rum

Just stir ingredients together with $1/2$ cup cold water and toast.

››››› HBC Grog ‹‹‹‹‹

The Hudson Bay Company, the fur-trading empire that virtually ruled much of the American Northwest for over 300 years, packed 151-proof rum into the interior strictly for economic reasons. Half as much went twice as far. It's not a drink for the faint-hearted, but it's well known to make faint hearts strong.

> 1 lump sugar
> 2 jiggers (3 ounces) 151-proof rum

Put the sugar in an 8-ounce mug. Add 3/4 cup boiling water, rum, and stir. Sip contemplatively (do not operate any machinery or use sharp-edged tools while doing so or afterward).

⟩⟩⟩⟩⟩ Hot Buttered Rum ⟨⟨⟨⟨⟨

Hands down, the most popular drink in camps where it's cold or wet or snowing or blowing a half gale. Few people today have ever tried it, though it was a great favorite on the American colonial frontier. The hot mixture of carbohydrates (sugar and liquor) and fat (butter) is as warming as it is tasty.

> 1 teaspoon sugar or 1 tablespoon maple syrup
> 1 pat butter (unsalted real butter, not margarine)
> 1^1/2 jiggers (2^1/4 ounces) rum

Put the sugar in a large mug. Add the butter, rum, and 1 cup boiling water; stir (with a spruce twig, for effect). If you've got nutmeg in your spice kit, sprinkle on top.

⟩⟩⟩⟩⟩ Frugal Brugal ⟨⟨⟨⟨⟨
(from Nelson Bryant)

By any measure, Nelson Bryant, whose "Outdoors" column has been a fixture in the *New York Times* for more than 30 years, is America's most skillful, witty, and insightful outdoor writer. In a column entitled "Singing the Praises of a Frugal Brugal in the Birth of the Booze," he described the makings of this memorable rum cocktail.

"The Frugal Brugal," wrote Bryant, "is a morning potion designed to sweep doubt and indecision from one's mind and to turn the dreariest dawn into something bright and shining. The first sip set my teeth on edge and made my eyes water, the second was less onerous and the remainder of the drink seemed remarkably smooth, so smooth, indeed, that I volunteered to make biscuits for our deer-hunting party of seven."

2 parts grapefruit juice, unsweetened
1 part dry Brugal rum

Mix well and imbibe.

BOURBON WHISKEY

The Lewis and Clark expedition was the first major voyage of North American exploration to forsake rum in preference of whiskey. Not Old World whiskey made from rye, barley, or wheat, mind you, but true American-born corn whiskey. It's quite likely this was Lewis's decision (perhaps with a wink and a nod from his sponsor, President Thomas Jefferson). In first carrying the young nation's flag across the continent, he wanted every item presented or traded to the Indian tribes along the way—including the booze—to be distinctively American.

With everything else the expedition was toting, there was

little room for whiskey, however. Though expecting to be gone up to four years, Lewis embarked only 120 gallons for 33 men. Since the expedition mustered first at Nashville, this was most probably straight bourbon whiskey which, at the time, was routinely from 100 to as much as 160 proof. Whichever, Lewis wrote that he doled it out to the men "whenever the river or weather had been particularly wayward . . . and it soon produced the fiddle and . . . much hilarity." The stuff mixed as well with the silt water of the Missouri as the spring waters of the Rockies. To give it an extra kick, it was sometimes mixed with blackstrap molasses into a drink called "skull-pop" or "skull varnish."

Today, a bottle of bonded Kentucky Straight Bourbon whiskey is hard to beat on a hunting, fishing, or camping trip. Amber colored and full bodied, with the aroma of oak, nothing complements a campfire and branch water better. The really good stuff—aged 15 years—is the smoothest, mellowest thing you can carry into the woods short of a down sleeping bag. And in all likelihood, you won't have to carry it out.

Personally, I believe it's best drunk straight or mixed with a modicum (a one-to-one measure) of water. There are a number of other time-honored ways, however, to take your bourbon in camp.

>>>>> Mint Julep <<<<<

You don't need a silver mug for this Kentucky kicker; a plain tin or enameled camp mug will do fine. It's best with ice, but just as good without. Mint is often found growing wild on stream banks.

3 to 4 mint leaves
1 tablespoon sugar
1^1/$_2$ jiggers (2^1/$_4$ ounces) bourbon

In a mug, muddle (mash) the mint and sugar with 2 table-spoons water. Fill the mug with crushed ice (if iceless, use ^{1}/$_2$ cup cold water instead), add the bourbon, and stir until the outside of the mug is cold and beaded with condensation.

⟩⟩⟩⟩⟩ Hot Brick Toddy ⟨⟨⟨⟨⟨

Like its rum cousin, this toddy is an antidote for cold weather and low morale. It's a bit more authoritative, however, because it's mixed in a short whiskey glass instead of a mug, and so contains less water.

1 teaspoon butter
1 teaspoon sugar
3 pinches cinnamon
1 jigger (1^1/$_2$ ounces) bourbon

Put the butter, sugar, and cinnamon in a whiskey glass. Add 2 tablespoons boiling water and stir until the butter and sugar dissolve. Add the bourbon; fill the remainder of the glass with boiling water, stir, and sip.

››››› Camp Old-fashioned ‹‹‹‹‹

While this is better shaken with or poured over ice, it's just as good in the woods muddled, stirred, and served without. Here's the ice-free version.

1 teaspoon sugar
Dash of bitters
1 or 2 orange slices
2 jiggers (3 ounces) bourbon

In a glass or mug, combine the sugar, bitters, orange slices, and 1 tablepoon of water. Muddle (mash) together. Add the bourbon, cover the glass, and shake well. Drink as is or, if you're fussy, strain with whatever is handy (clean bandanna, mosquito net, colander).

››››› Little Big Muddy ‹‹‹‹‹

Concocted in an outpost camp in approximation of old-time "skull pop."

Dash of bitters
1 teaspoon maple syrup
1$^{1}/_{2}$ jiggers (2$^{1}/_{4}$ ounces) bourbon

Stir the ingredients with ice, strain if desired, and serve.

›››› Bourbon Rickey ‹‹‹‹

A good end-of-the-fishing-day refresher, especially in summer.

$^1/_2$ lime
1 jigger ($1^1/_2$ ounces) bourbon
Soda water

Squeeze the juice from the lime into a glass; reserve the rind. Add bourbon and ice cubes, fill the glass with soda water, drop in the reserved lime rind, and stir.

›››› Kentucky Colonel Cocktail ‹‹‹‹

Mixing the liqueur of Benedictine monks with the liquor of Kentucky colonels beggars the imagination. But it turns out to be a good fit.

$^1/_2$ ounce Benedictine
1 jigger ($1^1/_2$ ounces) bourbon

Stir liqueur and liquor together with ice, then strain into a glass.

How Much to Take

Most liquor, when served straight, is poured by the shot glass, which contains 1 ounce of booze. Most cocktails, on the other hand, are poured by the jigger, which contains $1^1/_2$ ounces of booze. Depending upon the number of drinkers in your party, duration of the trip, and the conviviality you wish to dispense each evening at cocktail hour, standard-size liquor bottles yield the following (each jigger will make one cocktail):

$^1/_2$ pint (250 ml) = 8 ounces (or shots) = about 5 jiggers
$^3/_4$ pint (375 ml) = 12 ounces = 8 jiggers
1 pint (500 ml) = 16 ounces = about 11 jiggers
1 fifth (750 ml) = 25.6 ounces = 17 jiggers
1 quart (1 liter) = 32 ounces = 21 jiggers
$^1/_2$ gallon (1.75 liters) = 64 ounces = 43 jiggers

How to Take It

Leave all glass bottles or glass-lined flasks at home. Glass is obscenely heavy, not to mention breakable. Decant your libation into a sturdy screw-top, polycarbonate plastic bottle. Nalgene bottles (in 8-, 16-, or 32-ounce sizes) are highly recommended. Before they got into the outdoor recreation business, Nalge made heavy-duty containers for a Pandora's boxcar of caustic, noxious, poisonous chemicals, so their stuff's practically indestructible. These bottles have been widely copied—REI, Outdoor Products, and others make them in a wide variety of sizes and colors. Most all of these polycarb bottles come with a two- or three-thread screw top, secured to the bottle with a collar-and-strap arrangement, so there's no chance of losing the top or spilling a drop of your precious beverage. Neither will the hard polycarbonate plastic affect its taste or aroma.

Do not for a moment consider decanting good wine or liquor into aluminum canteens or soft (collapsible) plastic containers. They will impact taste and aroma.

◄◄◄ CAMP COOK'S DIRECTORY ►►►

I started cooking with a Boy Scout mess kit and a knife-fork-and-spoon set. Nowadays, I seem to possess everything from mini espresso makers to folding spatulas, from iron skillets to titanium pots, and one-burner stoves to portable camp kitchens. It's not overkill: every piece serves its particular purpose, not least of which is making the camp cook's life easier.

There's a fantastic range of camp cookware and food out there today, designed to meet virtually any camping need, whether you're in Aconcagua or the Adirondacks. You're sure to find whatever you need from the following suppliers. The list is representative, but by no means comprehensive.

FULL LINE: CAMP COOKWARE AND STOVES

Bass Pro Shops
www.basspro.com
(800) 976–6344
Springfield, MO

Brunton
www.brunton.com
(800) 443–4871
Riverton, NY

Cabela's

www.cabelas.com

(800) 237–4444

Oshkosh, NE

Over 40 years outfitting hunters, anglers, and campers for the great outdoors. Cooking ranges, portable camp kitchens, knife sets, meat grinders, meat slicers, sausage stuffers, food dehydraters, vacuum sealers, smokers, turkey fryers, apple and wine presses, wine-making kits, beer-brewing kits, thermoses, coffee pots, and cookware.

Campmor

www.campmor.com

(800) 226–7667

North Paramus, NJ

Full-range camping supplier. For camp cooking: cook kits, mess kits, camp stoves, cast-iron cookware, camp utensils, cups, plates, and bowls, Dutch ovens, and freeze-dried foods.

Coleman

www.coleman.com

(800) 835–3278

Wichita, KS

The granddaddy of camping supplies. Famous for their gas lanterns and coolers, they offer a comprehensive range of camp cookware: far too comprehensive to note here. Just note: if you need it for camp, Coleman probably has it. From the commonplace—aluminum cook sets—to the sublime—*unreadable* hot water heaters and coffee makers.

GSI Outdoors

www.gsioutdoors.com

(800) 704–4474

Spokane Valley, WA

MSR (Mountain Safety Research)
www.msrgear.com
(800) 531–9500
Seattle, WA
High-quality, superlatively designed and ruggedly made
cookware. MSR's line of camp stoves and cook sets is mostly
"expedition grade"—built for lightness and durability.
Expensive, but good stuff.

REI (Recreational Equipment Inc.)
www.REI.com
(800) 426–4840
Sumner, WA
A personal favorite, offers a full range of cookware suitable
for backpacking, canoeing, ski trekking, and car camping.
Available in a wide price range: from middle-of-the-road steel
cook sets to high-tech titanium ones. A cooperative where
members earn discounts and access to special sales.

Snow Peak
www.snowpeak.co.jp
(503) 697–3330
Clackamas, OR

TexSport
www.texsport.net
(877) 664–8444

CAST-IRON CAMP COOKWARE

BBQ
www.bbq.com
(877) 743–2269
Baton Rouge, LA

Camp Chef
www.campchef.com
(800) 650–2433
Logan, UT

Lodge
www.lodgemfg.com
(423) 837–7181
South Pittsburgh, TN
The first name in American cast-iron cookware. Family-owned and operated since 1896, it offers the most extensive line on the market.

COOLERS

Coleman
www.coleman.com
(800) 835–3278
Wichita, KS
The undisputed cooler king. They offer everything from personal-size coolers (nine models) to massive 150-quart marine coolers—with more than 30 other makes and models in between. Their Xtreme cooler models keep ice up to five days at temperatures up to 100°F.

Igloo Products
www.igloocoolers.com
Shelton, CT
Makers of a line of personal, full-size, and mega-size (120 and 150 quart) ice chests and coolers.

Thermos
www.thermos.com
(800) 831–9242
Rolling Meadows, IL

Thermos has been around since 1904. Nowadays, they're probably most noted for their extensive line of soft coolers, designed to keep canned beverages cold, and for their containers to keep things hot.

PORTABLE CAMP KITCHENS AND GRUB BOXES

Beaver Tree Kitchen
www.beavertree.com
Fall Creek, WI
The old-fashioned "grub box," the carry-all in which all cook gear was toted to camp, is still very much alive. Beaver Tree makes a rugged, lightweight one of rigid plastic, compartmentalized to accommodate pots, pans, and utensils. When opened, the top shelf accommodates a two-burner camp stove and its lid doubles as a sink.

Cabela's
www.cabelas.com
(800) 237–4444
Oshkosh, NE
Offers a 25-pound portable folding field kitchen that features a lantern/utensil holder, work surface, cutting board, shelves to accommodate a camp stove and camp cooler, and a food storage shelf.

E-Z Camping
(800) 535–6291
San Antonio, TX
E-Z offers a fully stocked, deluxe grub box. Made of heavy-gauge steel, it's compartmentalized and features internal turntables and a magnetic utensil rack. It comes packed with a coffeepot; three kettles; three mixing bowls; a frying pan; and plates, bowls, cups, and utensils for six campers.

GSI Outdoors
www.gisoutdoors.com
(800) 704–4474
Spokane Valley, WA
Definitely an item only for long-term, fixed camps, GSI's collapsible folding "kitchen station" is nonetheless an ingeniously designed piece of gadgetry. It erects into an L-shaped kitchen featuring a double sink, detachable cutting boards, utensil and lantern rack, hanging cupboards, and wire shelves for storing pots and pans.

CORNMEAL AND GRITS

Anson Mills
www.ansonmills.com
(803) 457–4122
Columbia, SC
Famous for heirloom, stone-ground white and yellow grits.

Cane Creek Grist Mill
www.canecreekgristmill.com
Hohenwald, TN
Stone-ground cornmeal and stone-ground wheat, rye, and buckwheat flour.

Edwards Mill
www.cofo.edu
(800) 222–6525
Point Lookout, MO
Yellow cornmeal and grits.

Falls Mill
E-mail: fallsmill@tnco.net
Belvidere, TN

Genuine waterwheel-powered, stone-ground cornmeal, grits, and flour. Mail order only.

Hoppin' John's
www.hoppinjohns.com
(800) 828–4412
Stone-ground cornmeal, grits, and flour.

Kenyon Cornmeal Company
www.kenyonsgristmill.com
(800) 753–6966
West Kingston, RI
Johnnycake white cornmeal, blue cornmeal (very hard to find), Kamut wheat flour, and brown rice flour.

Weisenberger Mills
www.weisenberger.com
(800) 643–8678
Midway, KY
Stone-ground white and yellow grits, hush puppy mix, fish batter mix, white cornbread mix, yellow corn muffin mix.

COUNTRY HAM, BACON, AND SAUSAGE
S. Wallace Edwards & Son
www.virginiatraditions.com
(800) 222–4267
Surry, VA
Traditional dry-cured, hardwood-smoked Virginia hams.

Hoffman's Quality Meats
www.info@hoffmanmeats.com
(800) 356–3193
Hagerstown, MD

Dry-cured, white hickory-smoked country ham, bacon, and sausage.

New Braunfels Smokehouse
www.nbsmokehouse.com
(800) 537–6932
New Braunfels, TX
Texas-style cured meats, including smoked ham, bacon, sausage; smoked turkey; peppered beef jerky.

Nueske's Meat Products
www.nueske.com
(800) 392–2266
Wittenberg, WI
Midwestern-style applewood-smoked ham, bacon, sausage, and poultry.

Oscar's Smokehouse
www.oscarssmokedmeats.com
(800) 627–3431
Warrensburg, NY
The place for bacon of all kinds: slab, Canadian, English, and Irish bacon—even beef brisket bacon. All-natural. Hickory and applewood smoked.

Ruef's Smoked Meats
E-mail: bruef@mail.tds.met
(608) 527–2554
New Giarus, WI
Specializing in homemade smoked beef and pork sausages. Oak and hickory smoked.

Smithfield Foods
www.smithfieldhams.com
(800) 926–8448 (for Smithfield, Luter's, and Gray &
Jordan's brand hams)
(800) 292–2773 (for Basse's, Gwaltney, and Williamsburg
brand hams)
Smithfield, VA
The oldest, perhaps most renowned of American country
hams. Dry-cured, oak or hickory smoked, and aged a minimum of 180 days.

Williams of Vermont
www.sover.net/~rosemary
(802) 447–0373
Bennington, VT
Corncob- and apple-smoked ham, bacon, and turkey.

DRIED NATURAL SOUPS

Cache Lake
www.cachelake.com
(800) 442–0852
Bemidji, MN
Good line of quick-cooking (20 minutes), "canoe country"
soups in hefty portions, including wild rice, leek and potato,
cheesy vegetable chowder, and Minnesota minestrone.

Fantastic Foods
www.fantasticfoods.com
(800) 288–1089
Napa, CA
One of the nation's leading natural (organic) food compa-
nies. Dried soups include black bean, lentil, couscous,
Spanish rice and beans, split pea, and others.

Harmony House Foods
www.harmonyhousefoods.com
(252) 746–7687
Winterville, NC
Extensive line of dehyrated additive-free soups includes split pea, lentil and barley, barley and mushroom, navy bean, black bean, and more. Just add water and cook for 20 minutes. Also sells a comprehensive range of dehydrated veggies: broccoli, cabbage, carrots, celery, corn, green beans, leeks, mushrooms, onions, peas, peppers, potatoes, spinach, and tomatoes.

Mary Jane's Farm Products
www.maryjanesfarm.com
(888) 750–6004
Moscow, ID
Quick-cooking, 100 percent organic dehydrated soups, including corn and bean chowder, creamy potato, curried lentil bisque, peasant tomato, and others. Also sells dehydrated entrées, side dishes, vegetables, and desserts.

Taste Adventure
www.tasteadventure.com
(800) 874–0883
Natural, quick-cooking (20 minutes), low-sodium soups include minestrone, navy bean, and split pea.

WILD RICE

Christmas Point Wild Rice Co.
www.christmaspoint.com
(218) 828–0603
Harvested by hand in a canoe, the traditional Indian way, from remote lakes in northern Minnesota, Christmas Point wild rice is the genuine article. The company also sells cultivated, machine-harvested wild rice.

Far North Wild Rice
www.wildrice.mb.ca/
(204) 687–3631
Flin Flon, Manitoba
Certified wild organic rice harvested in Canada's Churchill River country.

Gibbs Wild Rice
Email: gibbsrice@succeed.net
(800) 824–4932
Live Oak, CA
Cultivated wild rice, less expensive than the "wild thing," but still good.

McFadden Farm
www.mcfaddenfarm.com
(800) 544–8230
Potter Valley, CA
Cultivated wild rice.

Ramy Wild Rice Co.
www.ramywildrice.com
(800) 658–7269
Ramy has been selling 100 percent naturally grown and traditionally harvested wild rice since 1932.

DRIED HEIRLOOM BEANS
Phipps County Store and Farm
www.phippscounty.com
(650) 879–0787
Pescadero, CA
Not your grandfather's beans—more like your great-grandfather's beans. Perfect for rediscovering the goodness of old-fashioned camp bean dishes. Native American beans are

pesticide-free and planted, harvested, processed, and packaged by hand. Phipps offers an astounding variety, among them appaloosa, buckskin, cranberry, desert pebble, Jacob's cattle, piebald, painted pony, red-speckled Dixie, and scarlet runner beans. Gourmet fare of the highest order.

◄◄◄ BIBLIOGRAPHY ►►►

Angier, Bradford. *Home in Your Pack.* Harrisburg, PA: Stackpole Books, 1965.

Bakeless, John. *America as Seen by Its First Explorers.* New York: Dover Publications, 1961.

———. *Daniel Boone: Master of the Wilderness.* Lincoln, NE: University of Nebraska Press, 1989 (first published in 1939).

Bean, L. L. *Hunting-Fishing and Camping.* Saybrook, CT: Applewood Books, 1993 (first published in 1942).

Birk, Douglas. *John Sayer's Snake River Journal 1804–05.* Minneapolis, MN: Institute for Minnesota Archaeology, 1989.

Bryant, Nelson. *Outdoors: A Personal Selection from Twenty Years of Columns from The New York Times.* New York: Simon and Schuster, 1990.

Burand, Jean. *Alaska's Game Is Good Food.* Anchorage, AK: University of Alaska, 1971.

Catlin, George. *Letters and Notes on the Manners, Customs and Conditions of North American Indians.* New York: Dover Publications, 1973 (first published in 1844).

Davidson, James West, and John Rugge. *The Complete Wilderness Paddler.* New York: Vintage, 1982.

DeVoto, Bernard. *The Journals of Lewis and Clark.* Boston: Houghton Mifflin Company, 1953.

Ferber, Peggy (Editor). *Mountaineering: The Freedom of the Hills.* Seattle: The Mountaineers Books, 1974.

Fletcher, Colin. *The Complete Walker.* New York: Alfred A. Knopf, 1974.

———. *The Man Who Walked Through Time.* New York: Random House, 1967.

Fletcher, Colin. *The Thousand-Mile Summer.* New York: Howell-North Books, 1964.

Haber, Barbara. *From Hardtack to Home Fries: An Uncommon History of American Cooks and Meals.* New York: The Free Press, 2002.

Hawke, David. *Everyday Life in Early America.* New York: Harper & Row, 1988.

Hemingway, Ernest. *The Nick Adams Stories.* New York: Scribners, 1972 (first published in 1927).

Hendricksson, John (Editor). *North Writers: A Strong Woods Collection.* Minneapolis, MN: University of Minnesota Press, 1981.

Herter, Berthe, and George Herter. *Bull Cook and Authentic Historical Recipes and Practices.* Waseca, MN: Herter's Inc., 1964.

Hoffman, Kathryn, and Kate Moss. *The Backcountry Housewife: A Study of 18ᵗʰ Century Foods.* Gastonia, NC: Schiele Museum, 1994.

Kylloe, Ralph. *Fishing Camps.* Salt Lake City: Gibbs-Smith, 2002.

Lehmberg, Paul. *In the Strong Woods: A Season Alone in the North Country.* New York: St. Martin's Press, 1980.

Luchetti, Cathy. *Home On the Range: A Culinary History of the American West.* New York: Willard Books, 1993.

Luxenberg, Larry. *Walking the Appalachian Trail.* Mechanicsburg, PA: Stackpole Books, 1994.

Mack, Norman (Editor). *Back to Basics: How to Learn and Enjoy Traditional American Skills.* Pleasantville, NY: The Reader's Digest Association, 1981.

Mackenzie, Sir Alexander. *Voyages from Montreal Through the Continent of North America.* New York: AMS Press, 1973 (first published in 1797).

Marcy, Captain Randolph B. *The Prairie Traveler: A Handbook for Overland Expeditions.* Cambridge: Applewood Books, 1988 (first published in 1859).

Margolis, Carolyn, and Herman Viola. *Seeds of Change: 500 Years Since Columbus.* Washington: Smithsonian Institution Press, 1991.

Mason, Bill. *Song of the Paddle: An Illustrated Guide to Wilderness Camping.* Toronto: Key Porter Books, 1988.

McGee, Harold. *On Food and Cooking.* New York: Scribners, 1984.

McManners, Hugh. *The Complete Wilderness Training Book: Field Skills for Adventure in the Outdoors.* New York: Dorling Kindersley, 1994.

McPhee, John. *The Survival of the Bark Canoe.* New York: Farrar, Straus and Giroux, 1975.

Mead, Robert. *The Canoer's Bible.* Garden City, NY: Doubleday & Company, 1976.

Miracle, Leonard. *Sportsman's Camping Guide.* New York: Harper & Row, 1965.

Mirsky, Jeannette. *The Westward Crossings: Balboa, Mackenzie, Lewis and Clark*. New York: Alfred A. Knopf, 1946.

Mother Earth News (Editors). *The Rural Living Handbook: Guide to Practical Country Skills*. New York: Fireside/Simon and Schuster, 1989.

Muir, John. *My First Summer In the Sierra*. New York: Penguin Press, 1987 (first published in 1911).

Olson, Sigurd. *The Lonely Land*. New York: Alfred A. Knopf, 1961.

Ornig, Joseph. *My Last Chance to Be A Boy: Theodore Roosevelt's South American Expedition of 1913–1914*. Baton Rouge, LA: Louisiana State University Press, 1994.

Osborne, Jean. *Gourmet Camping: A Menu Cookbook and Travel Guide for Campers, Canoeists, Cyclists, and Skiers*. Brandon, MS: Quail Ridge Press, 1988.

Pearson, Claudia. *NOLS (National Outdoor Leadership Schools) Cookery*. Mechanicsburg, PA: Stackpole Books, 2004.

Prater, Yvonne, and Ruth Mendenhall. *Gorp, Glop and Glue Stew*. Seattle: The Mountaineers Books, 1982.

Ross, Cindy, and Todd Gladfelter. *A Hiker's Companion: 12,000 Miles of Trail-Tested Wisdom*. Seattle: The Mountaineers Books, 1993.

Rutstrum, Calvin. *Chips From A Wilderness Log*. New York: Scarborough Books/Stein and Day, 1982.

Saijo, Albert. *The Backpacker*. San Francisco: 101 Productions, 1977.

Satterfield, Archie. *The Eddie Bauer Guide to Backpacking*. Reading, MA: Addison-Wesley Publishing Company, 1983.

Sears, George Washington [Nessmuk]. *Woodcraft and Camping*. New York: Dover Publications, 1963 (first published in 1920).

Schneider, Paul. *The Adirondacks: A History of America's First Wilderness*. New York: Henry Holt and Company, 1997.

Simer, Peter, and John Sullivan. *The National Outdoor Leadership School's Wilderness Guide*. New York: Simon and Schuster, 1983.

Swell, Barbara. *Log Cabin Cooking*. Asheville, NC: Native Ground Music, 1996.

Teller, Walter. *On the River: A Variety of Canoe and Small Boat Voyages*. Dobbs Ferry, NY: Sheridan House, 1988.

Thomas, Dian. *Roughing It Easy: A Unique Ideabook for Camping and Cooking*. Salt Lake City: Dian Thomas Company, 1994.

Thoreau, Henry David. *The Maine Woods*. New York: Apollo Editions, 1966 (first published in 1834).

Toussaint-Samat, Maguelonne. *A History of Food*. Paris: Bordas, 1987.

U.S. Army. *U.S. Army Survival Manual.* New York: Dorset Press, 1991 (reprint of Department of the Army Field Manual 21–76).

Viehman, John (Editor). *Trailside's Trail Food.* Emmaus, PA: Rodale Press, 1993.

Wescott, David. *Camping In the Old Style.* Salt Lake City: Gibbs-Smith, 2000.

Williams, Jaqueline. *Wagon Wheel Kitchens: Food on the Oregon Trail.* Lawrence, KS: University Press of Kansas, 1993.

Wiseman, John. *The SAS Survival Handbook.* London: Harvill/HarperCollins, 1992.

Watson, Kim (Editor). *Wild Things: Recipes From the Wild.* Atikokan, ONT: Friends of the Atikokan Centennial Museum, 2003.

Woodruff, Woody. *Cooking the Dutch Oven Way.* Guilford, CT: Globe Pequot Press, 2000.

◄◄◄ INDEX ►►►